Rainer Buchty, Jan-Philipp Weiß (eds.)

High-performance and Hardware-aware Computing

Proceedings of the Second International Workshop on New Frontiers in High-performance and Hardware-aware Computing (HipHaC'11)

San Antonio, Texas, USA, February 2011
(In Conjunction with HPCA-17)

High-performance and Hardware-aware Computing

Proceedings of the Second International Workshop on New Frontiers in High-performance and Hardware-aware Computing (HipHaC'11)

San Antonio, Texas, USA, February 2011
(In Conjunction with HPCA-17)

Rainer Buchty
Jan-Philipp Weiß
(eds.)

 Scientific Publishing

Impressum

Karlsruher Institut für Technologie (KIT)
KIT Scientific Publishing
Straße am Forum 2
D-76131 Karlsruhe
www.ksp.kit.edu

KIT – Universität des Landes Baden-Württemberg und nationales
Forschungszentrum in der Helmholtz-Gemeinschaft

KIT Scientific Publishing 2011
Print on Demand

ISBN 978-3-86644-626-7

Organization

Workshop Organizers:

Rainer Buchty

Eberhard Karls University Tübingen, Germany,

& Karlsruhe Institute of Technology, Germany

Jan-Philipp Weiß

Karlsruhe Institute of Technology, Germany

Steering Committee:

Vincent Heuveline

Karlsruhe Institute of Technology, Germany

Wolfgang Karl

Karlsruhe Institute of Technology, Germany

Program Committee:

David A. Bader

Georgia Tech, Atlanta, USA

Michael Bader

Univ. Stuttgart, Germany

Mladen Berekovic

Univ. Braunschweig, Germany

Alan Berenbaum

SMSC, USA

Martin Bogdan

Univ. Leipzig, Germany

Dominik Göddeke

TU Dortmund, Germany

Georg Hager

Univ. Erlangen, Germany

Vincent Heuveline

Karlsruhe Institute of Technology, Germany

Eric d'Hollander

Ghent University, Belgium

Michael Hübner

Karlsruhe Institute of Technology, Germany

Ben Juurlink

TU Berlin, Germany

Wolfgang Karl

Karlsruhe Institute of Technology, Germany

Rainer Keller

HLRS, Stuttgart, Germany

Hiroaki Kobayashi

Tohoku University, Japan

Harald Köstler

Univ. Erlangen, Germany

Dieter an Mey

RWTH Aachen, Germany

Andy Nisbet

Manchester Metropolitan University, UK

Christian Perez

INRIA, France

Preface

High-performance system architectures are increasingly exploiting heterogeneity: multi- and manycore-based systems are complemented by coprocessors, accelerators, and reconfigurable units providing huge computational power. However, applications of scientific interest (e.g. in high-performance computing and numerical simulation) are not yet ready to exploit the available high computing potential. Different programming models, non-adjusted interfaces, and bandwidth bottlenecks complicate holistic programming approaches for heterogeneous architectures. In modern microprocessors, hierarchical memory layouts and complex logics obscure predictability of memory transfers or performance estimations.

For efficient implementations and optimal results, underlying algorithms and mathematical solution methods have to be adapted carefully to architectural constraints like fine-grained parallelism and memory or bandwidth limitations that require additional communication and synchronization. Currently, a comprehensive knowledge of underlying hardware is therefore mandatory for application programmers. Hence, there is strong need for virtualization concepts that free programmers from hardware details, maintaining best performance and enable deployment in heterogeneous and reconfigurable environments.

The Second International Workshop on New Frontiers in High-performance and Hardware-aware Computing (HipHaC'11) – held in conjunction with the 17th IEEE International Symposium on High-Performance Computer Architecture (HPCA-17) – aims at combining new aspects of parallel, heterogeneous, and reconfigurable system architectures with concepts of high-performance computing and, particularly, numerical solution methods. It brings together international researchers of all affected fields to discuss issues of high-performance computing on emerging hardware architectures, ranging from architecture work to programming and tools.

The workshop organizers would therefore like to thank the HPCA-17 Workshop Chair for giving us the chance to host this workshop in conjunction with one of the world's finest conferences on high-performance architectures – and of course all the people who made this workshop finally happen. Thanks to the many contributors submitting exciting and novel work, HipHaC'11 will reflect a broad range of issues on architecture design, algorithm implementation, and application optimization.

Karlsruhe, January 2011

Rainer Buchty[1,2] & Jan-Philipp Weiß[2]
[1] Eberhard Karls University Tübingen
[2] Karlsruhe Institute of Technology (KIT)

Table of Content

Convey HC-1 Hybrid Core Computer – The Potential of FPGAs in Numerical Simulation

Werner Augustin, Jan-Philipp Weiss
Engineering Mathematics and Computing Lab (EMCL)
SRG New Frontiers in High Performance Computing
Exploiting Multicore and Coprocessor Technology
Karlsruhe Institute of Technology, Germany
werner.augustin@kit.edu, jan-philipp.weiss@kit.edu

Vincent Heuveline
Engineering Mathematics and Computing Lab (EMCL)
Karlsruhe Institute of Technology, Germany
vincent.heuveline@kit.edu

Abstract—The Convey HC-1 Hybrid Core Computer brings FPGA technologies closer to numerical simulation. It combines two types of processor architectures in a single system. Highly capable FPGAs are closely connected to a host CPU and the accelerator-to-memory bandwidth has remarkable values. Reconfigurability by means of pre-defined application-specific instruction sets called personalities have the appeal of optimized hardware configuration with respect to application characteristics. Moreover, Convey's solution eases the programming effort considerably. In contrast to hardware-centric and time-consuming classical coding of FPGAs, a dual-target compiler interprets pragma-extended C/C++ or Fortran code and produces implementations running on both, host and accelerator. In addition, a global view of host and device memory is provided by means of a cache-coherent shared virtual memory space.

In this work we analyze Convey's programming paradigm and the associated programming effort, and we present practical results on the HC-1. We consider vectorization strategies for the single and double precision vector personalities and a suite of basic numerical routines. Furthermore, we assess the viability of the Convey HC-1 Hybrid Core Computer for numerical simulation.

Keywords-FPGA, Convey HC-1, reconfigurable architectures, high-performance heterogeneous computing, coherent memory system, performance analysis, BLAS

I. INTRODUCTION

Field Programmable Gate Arrays (FPGAs) have their main pillar and standing in the domain of embedded computing. Application-specific designs implemented by hardware description languages (HDL) like VHDL and Verilog [1], [2] make them a perfect fit for specific tasks. From a software-oriented programmer's point of view FPGA's capabilities are hidden behind an alien hardware design development cycle. Although there are some C-to-HDL tools like ROCCC, Impulse C or Handle-C [3] available, viability and translation efficiency for realistic code scenarios still have to be proven.

For several years, FPGAs have not been interesting for numerical simulations due to their limited capabilities and resource requirements for double precision floating point arithmetics. But following Moore's law and with increased FPGA sizes more and more area is becoming available for computing. Moreover, further rates of increase are expected to outpace those of common multicore CPUs. For a general deployment and in particular for numerical simulation FPGAs are very attractive from further points of view: run-time configurability is an interesting topic for applications with several phases of communication and computation and might be considered for adaptive numerical methods. In addition, energy efficiency is a great concern in high performance computing and FPGA technology is a possible solution approach. The main idea of FPGAs is to build one's own parallel fixed-function units according to the special needs of the underlying application.

Currently, numerical simulation adopts all kinds of emerging technologies. In this context, a trend towards heterogeneous platforms has become apparent [4]. Systems accelerated by *graphics processing units* (GPUs) offer unrivaled computing power but often suffer from slow interconnection via PCIe links. The idea to connect FPGAs via socket replacements closer to CPUs is nothing new (cf. technologies from Nallatech, DRC, XtremeData) – but the software concept offered by Convey is revolutionary [5]. A related FPGA platform is Intel's Atom reconfigurable processor – an embedded single board computer based on the Intel Atom E600C processor paired with an Altera FPGA in a single package. Here, both entities communicate via PCIe-x1 links. Former hybrid CPU-FPGA machines were the Cray XD1 [6] and the SGI RC100.

In this work we outline the hardware and software architecture of the Convey HC-1 Hybrid Core Computer. We analyze Convey's programming concept and assess the functionalities and capabilities of Convey's single and double precision vector personalities. Furthermore, we evaluate the viability of the Convey HC-1 Hybrid Core Computer for numerical simulation by means of selected numerical kernels that are well-known building blocks for higher-level numerical schemes, solvers, and applications. Some performance results on the HC-1 can be found in [7]. Our work puts more emphasis on floating point kernels relevant for numerical simulation. Stencil applications on the HC-1 are also considered in [8].

II. HARDWARE CONFIGURATION OF THE CONVEY HC-1

The Convey HC-1 Hybrid Core Computer is an example of a heterogeneous computing platform. By its hybrid setup, specific application needs can either be handled by an x86-64 dual-core CPU or by the application-adapted FPGAs. All

1

computational workloads are processed by a 2.13GHz Intel Xeon 5138 dual-core host CPU and by the *application engines* (AE), a set of four Xilinx Virtex 5 LX330 FPGAs. Two more V5LX110 FPGAs implement the host interface – the *application engine hub* (AEH) – for data transfers and control flow exchange between host and device, and eight V5LX155 FPGAs build the eight accelerator's memory controllers. Data transfers are communicated via the CPU's front-side bus (FSB), Intel's aging technology. Across the whole system a cache-coherent shared virtual memory system is provided that allows to access data in the CPU's memory and in the accelerator device memory. However, the system incorporates a ccNUMA system where proper data placement is performance-critical. In our system the host CPU is equipped with 16x667MHz FBDIMMs providing 16 GB of memory and a theoretical bandwidth of 8 GB/s. On the device 16 DDR2 memory channels feed Convey's special 16x667MHz Scatter-Gather-DIMMs with 8 GB device memory and a theoretical peak bandwidth of 80 GB/s. The fundamental advantage of this memory configuration is that non-unit strides have no drawback on the effective bandwidth. All data can be accessed with 8 byte granularity. Functional units on the FPGAs are implemented by logic synthesis by means of Convey's personalities [5]. The single precision vector personality provides a load-store vector architecture with 32 function pipes, each one containing a vector register file and four fused-multiply-add (FMA) vector units for exploiting data parallelism by means of vectorization. Furthermore, out-of-order execution provides a means for instruction-level parallelism. While the clock rate of the FPGAs is undisclosed, the peak GFlop/s rate is expected to be about 80 GFlop/s for single precision and 40 GFlop/s for double precision. The most accented difference of the FPGA accelerator memory subsystem is that there are no caches and no local memory available. All block-RAM on the FPGA is not accessible by the user (unless custom personalities and FPGA designs are created that support this feature). The whole system consumes about 650-850 Watt (depending on the actual workload). A sketch of the HC-1's hardware configuration is shown in Figure 1.

In comparison to other accelerators – like e.g. recent GPUS or the Cell BE – the HC-1 offers lower peak performance and lower bandwidth. But in contrast, fast device memory can be configured up to 128 GB in size and is not limited to a few GB as on GPUs. Furthermore, Convey's technology and its future development will possibly allow fast cluster-like connection between several FPGA-based entities. The latest Convey product, the HC-1ex was improved with newer Xilinx Virtex 6 FPGAs and an Intel 5408 Xeon quad-core processor.

III. CONVEY HC-1'S SOFTWARE ENVIRONMENT

Programming of FPGAs by means of HDL is a time-consuming and non-intuitive effort – and so FPGAs have been out of reach for many domain experts. With Convey's solution, FPGAs are now a viable alternative from a programming point of view. On the Convey HC-1, the CPU's capabilities are extended by application-specific

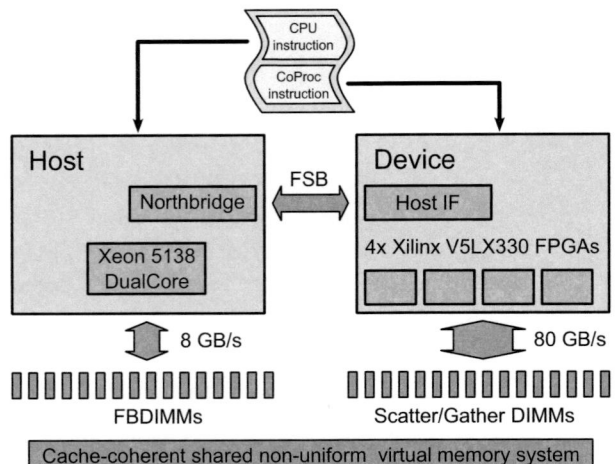

Fig. 1. Hardware Configuration of the Convey HC-1

instructions for the FPGAs [5]. However, the asymmetric computing platform is hidden by Convey's unified software interface. A single code base (C, C++ or Fortran) can be enhanced with pragmas to advise the compiler how to treat computations and data. In particular, code regions that should be executed on the FPGAs can be identified by inserting `#pragma cny begin_coproc / end_coproc`. Another possibility is to compile whole subroutines for the accelerator, or even to use compiler's capability for automatic identification of parts, that shall be offloaded to the FPGAs. Typical code sections are those suitable for vectorization, especially long loops. The compiler then produces a dual target executable, i.e. the code can be executed on both the CPU host (e.g. if the coprocessor is not available) and on the FPGA accelerator. Hence, a portable solution is created that can run on any x86 system. There are some restrictions to coprocessor code: it is not possible to do I/O, to make system calls or to call non-coprocessor functions. A compiler report gives details on the vectorization procedure. Specific pragmas give further hints for compiler-based optimizations.

Both memories on the host CPU and on the FPGA accelerator are combined into a common address space and data types are common across both entities. In order to prevent NUMA effects, placement of data can be controlled by pragmas. Data allocated in the CPU memory can be transferred to the accelerator with `#pragma cny migrate_coproc`. Dynamic and static memory on the FPGA device can be allocated directly via `#pragma cny_cp_malloc` and `#pragma cny coproc_mem` respectively. In case of memory migration whole memory pages are transferred. In order to avoid multiple transfers, several data objects should be grouped into larger structs.

The actual configuration of the FPGAs is represented by means of application-specific instruction sets called personalities. These personalities augment the host's x86-64 instruction set. This features allows adaptation and optimization of the hardware with respect to the specific needs of the underlying

2

algorithms. The user only has to treat an integrated instruction set controlled by pragmas and compiler settings. Convey offers a set of pre-defined personalities for single and double precision floating point arithmetics that turn the FPGAs into a soft-core vector processor. Furthermore, personalities for financial analytics and for proteomics are available. Currently, a finite difference personality for stencil computations is under development. The choice for a requested personality is specified at compile time by setting compiler flags. With Convey's personality development kit custom personalities can be developed by following the typical FPGA hardware design tool chain (requiring considerable effort and additional knowledge). Convey's *Software Performance Analysis Tool* (SPAT) gives insight into the system's actual runtime behavior and feedback on possible optimizations. The Convey Math Library (CML) provides tuned basic mathematical kernels. For our experiments we used the Convey64 Compiler Suite, Version 2.0.0.

IV. THE POTENTIAL OF FPGAS

FPGAs have been considered to be non-optimal for floating point number crunching. But FPGAs show particular benefits for specific workloads like processing complex mathematical expressions (logs, exponentials, transcendentals), performing bit operations (shifts, manipulations), and performing sort operations (string comparison, pattern recognition). Further benefits can be achieved for variable bit length of data types with reduced or increased precision, or for treating non-standard number formats (e.g. decimal representation). The latter points are exploited within Convey's personalities for financial applications and proteomics. Recently, Convey reported a remarkable speedup of 172 for the Smith-Waterman algorithm [9].

Pure floating point-based algorithms in numerical simulation are often limited by bandwidth constraints and low arithmetic intensity (ratio of flop per byte). The theoretical peak bandwidth of 80 GB/s on the Convey FPGA device goes along with a specific appeal in this context. However, memory accesses on the device are not cached. Hence, particular benefits are expected for kernels with limited data reuse like vector updates (SAXPY/DAXPY), scalar products (SDOT/DDOT) and sparse matrix-vector multiplications (SpMV). Convey's special Scatter-Gather DIMMs are well adapted to applications with irregular data access patterns where CPUs and GPUs typically show tremendous performance breakdowns.

V. PERFORMANCE EVALUATION

In order to assess the performance potential of Convey's FPGA platform for floating point-based computations in numerical simulation we analyze some basic numerical kernels and their performance behavior. In particular, we consider library-based kernels provided by the CML and hand-written, optimized kernels. By comparing both results we draw some conclusion on the capability of Convey's compiler. In all cases, vectorization of the code and NUMA-aware placement of data is crucial for performance. Without vectorization there is a

dramatic performance loss since scalar code for the accelerator is executed on the slow *application engine hub* (AEH) that builds the interface between host and accelerator device. If data is not located in the accelerator memory but is accessed in the host memory over the FSB, bandwidth and hence performance also drop considerably.

For our numerical experiments we consider some basic building blocks for high-level solvers, namely vector updates $z = ax + y$ (SAXPY/DAXPY in single and double precision), vector product $\alpha = x \cdot y$ (SDOT/DDOT), dense matrix-vector multiplication $y = Ax$ (SGEMV/DGEMV), dense matrix-matrix multiplication $C = AB$ (DGEMM/SGEMM), sparse matrix vector multiplication (SpMV), and stencil operations.

VI. VECTORIZATION AND OPTIMIZATION OF CODE

In order to exploit the full capabilities of the FPGA accelerator specific measures are necessary for code creation, for organizing data accesses, and to support the compiler for vectorizing code. Due to its nature as a low frequency, highly parallel vector architecture, performance on the Convey HC-1 heavily depends on the ability of the compiler to vectorize the code. One of the examples where this did not work out-of-the-box is dense matrix-vector multiplication SGEMV. The code snippet in Figure 2 shows a straightforward implementation. Here, the pragma cny no_loop_dep gives a hint to the compiler for vectorization that there are no data dependencies in the corresponding arrays.

```
void gemv(int length, float A[], float x[],
          float y[]){
  for( int i = 0; i < length; i++) {
    float sum = 0;
#pragma cny no_loop_dep(A, x, y)
    for( int j = 0; j < length; j++)
      sum += A[i*length+j] * x[j];
    y[i] = sum;
  }
}
```

Fig. 2. Straightforward implementation of dense matrix-vector multiplication (SGEMV)

Although the compiler claims to vectorize the inner loop, performance is only approx. 2 GFlop/s and by a factor of 7 below the performance of the CML math library version. The coprocessor instruction set supports vector reduction operations, but these seem to have a pretty high startup latency. The outer loop is not unrolled. Attempts to do that manually improved the performance somewhat, but introduced new performance degradations for certain vector lengths.

The solution lies in exploiting Convey's scatter-gather memory which allows for fast strided memory reads and therefore allows to change the loop ordering (see Figure 3). This gives considerably better results; performance improvements by loop reordering are detailed in Figure 4. For the reordered loops we consider three different memory allocation scenarios: dynamic memory allocated on the host and migrated with

3

Convey's pragma `cny migrate_coproc`, dynamic memory allocated on the device, and static memory allocated on the host and migrated to the device with the pragma mentioned above. Performance increases with vector length but has some oscillations. These results even outperform the CML CBLAS library implementation from Convey (cf. Figure 13).

```
void optimized_gemv(int length, float A[],
                    float x[], float y[]){
  for( int i = 0; i < length; i++ )
    y[i] = 0.0;
  for( int j = 0; j < length; j++ )
#pragma cny no_loop_dep(A, x, y)
    for( int i = 0; i < length; i++ )
      y[i] += A[i*length+j] * x[j];
}
```

Fig. 3. Dense matrix-vector multiplication (SGEMV) optimized by loop reordering

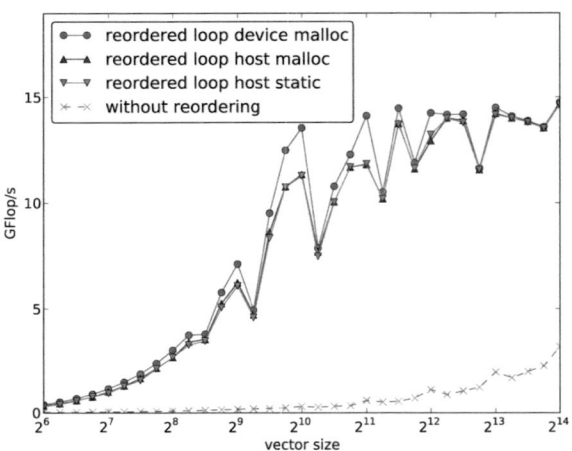

Fig. 4. Performance results and optimization for single precision dense matrix-vector multiplication (SGEMV) with and without loop reordering and for different memory allocation schemes; cf. Fig. 2 and Fig. 3

VII. PERFORMANCE RESULTS AND ANALYSIS

A. Device Memory Bandwidth for Different Access Patterns

Performance of numerical kernels is often influenced by the corresponding memory bandwidth for loading and storing data. For our memory bandwidth measurements we use the following memory access patterns that are characteristic of diverse kernels:

Sequential Read (SeRd):	$d[i] = s[i]$
Sequential Read Indexed (SeRdI):	$d[i] = s[seq[i]]$
Scattered Read Indexed (ScaRdI):	$d[i] = s[rnd[i]]$
Sequential Write (SeWr):	$d[i] = s[i]$
Sequential Write Indexed (SeWrI):	$d[seq[i]] = s[i]$
Scattered Write Indexed (ScaWrI):	$d[rnd[i]] = s[i]$

Here, $seq[i] = i$, $i = 1, \ldots, N$, is a sequential but indirect addressing and $rnd[i]$ is an indirect addressing by an arbitrary permutation of $[1, \ldots, N]$. Performance results for the described memory access patterns in single and double precision on the Convey HC-1, on a 2-way 2.53 GHz Intel Nehalem processor using 8 threads on 8 cores, on a single GPU of a NVIDIA Tesla S1070 system, and on a GTX 480 consumer GPU with the latest Fermi architecture are presented in Figure 5.

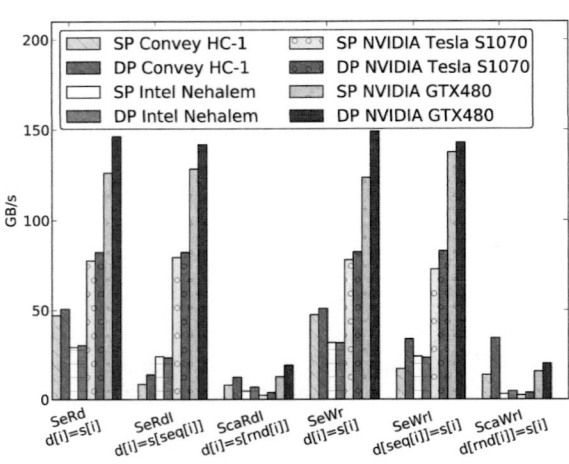

Fig. 5. Memory bandwidth for different memory access patterns on the Convey HC-1, on a 2-way 2.53 GHz Intel Nehalem system processor with 8 cores, on a single GPU of an NVIDIA Tesla S1070 system, and on an NVIDIA GTX480 consumer GPU

For the sequential indirect access, the CPU and GPU have built-in hardware mechanisms (caches for the CPU and memory coalescing for the GPU) to detect the access locality and therefore the performance does not decrease much while the HC-1 bandwidth already drops considerably. For the scattered read and write access, Convey's memory configuration gives better values than the Nehalem system and even outpaces the GTX 480 for scattered write in double precision. The Convey HC-1 not only has an about 60% percent higher peak memory bandwidth than the Nehalem system, but it really shows the potential of its scatter-gather capability when accessing random locations in memory. Here, traditional cache-based architectures typically perform poorly and at least the older generation of GPU systems has a breakdown by an order of magnitude. Newer GPU systems represented by the GTX 480 on the other hand have improved considerably.

B. Data-Transfers Between Host and Device

Because of the strong asymmetric NUMA-architecture of the HC-1 there are different methods to use main memory. Three of them are used in the following examples:

- dynamically allocate (malloc) and initialize on the host; use migration pragmas

4

- dynamically allocate (cny_cp_malloc) and initialize on the device
- statically allocate and initialize on the host; use migration pragmas

By initialization we mean the first touch of the data in memory. Because the Convey HC-1 is based on Intel's precedent technology of using the front-side bus (FSB) to connect memory to processors a major bottleneck is the data connection between host memory and device memory. Figure 6 shows a comparison between read bandwidth on the host and the device and the migration bandwidth over the HC-1's front side bus in GB/s. While read bandwidth on the device memory reaches almost 33 GB/s, the transfer over the FSB achieves only about 700 MB/s. This impedes fast switching between parts of an algorithm which perform well on the coprocessor and its vector units and other parts relying on the flexibility of high-clocked general purpose CPU. Compared to GPUs attached via PCIe, the FSB represents an even more narrow bottleneck.

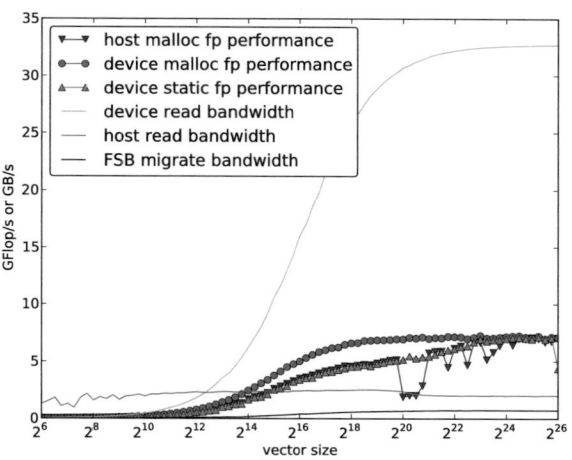

Fig. 6. Read bandwidth on host and device and migration bandwidth in GB/s on the Convey HC-1; Performance results in GFlop/s for the SAXPY vector update for different memory allocation schemes

Furthermore, Figure 6 depicts performance of the SAXPY in terms of GFlop/s (the unit on the y-axis has to be chosen correspondingly). For data originally allocated on the host and migrated to the device we observe some oscillations in the performance.

C. Avoiding Bank Conflicts with 31-31 Interleave

The scatter-gather memory configuration of the Convey HC-1 can be used in two different mapping modes:

- Binary interleave: traditional approach, parts of the address bitmap are mapped round-robin to different memory banks
- 31-31 interleave: modulo 31 mapping of parts of the address bitmap

Because in the 31-31 interleave mode the memory is divided into 31 groups of 31 banks, memory strides of powers of two and many other strides hit different banks and therefore do not suffer from memory bandwidth degradation. But to integrate this prime number scheme into a power of two dominated world, one of 32 groups and every 32th bank are not used resulting in a loss of some addressable memory and approximately 6% of peak memory bandwidth. In Figure 7 performance results for the SAXPY vector update are shown for both interleave options. For the SAXPY, binary memory interleave is slightly worse. Performance results for the CML DGEMM routine in Figure 8 show larger variations with 31-31 interleave. The DGEMM routine achieves about 36 GFlop/s and the SGEMM routine yields about 72 GFlop/s on our machine. In both cases this is roughly 90% of the estimated machine peak performance.

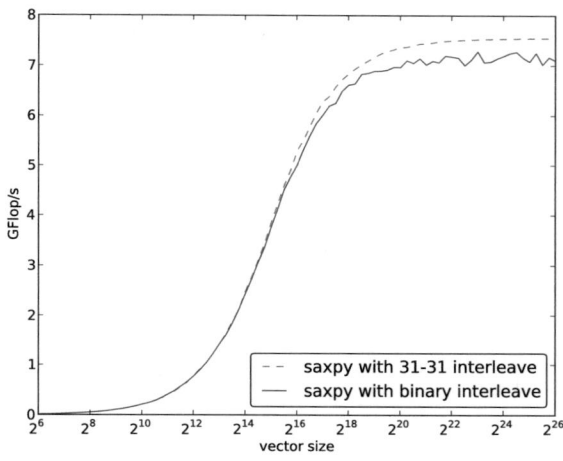

Fig. 7. Performance of SAXPY vector updates with 31-31 and binary interleave

D. BLAS Operations

Basic Linear Algebra Subprograms (BLAS) [10] are a collection and interface for basic numerical linear algebra routines. We use these routines for assessment of the HC-1 FPGA platform. We compare our own, straightforward implementations of BLAS-routines with those provided by Convey's Math Library (CML). Loop reordering techniques are applied for performance improvements. In the following examples we use the three different memory usage schemes detailed in Section VII-B. In all three cases initialization and migration costs are not considered in our measurements.

Data allocation on the host followed by migration routines or pragmas is not really a controllable and reliable procedure. From time to time considerable drops in performance are observed. So far, we could not identify a reasonable pattern or a satisfactory explanation for these effects. Our measurements are made using separate program calls for a set of parameters. When trying to measure by looping over different vector

5

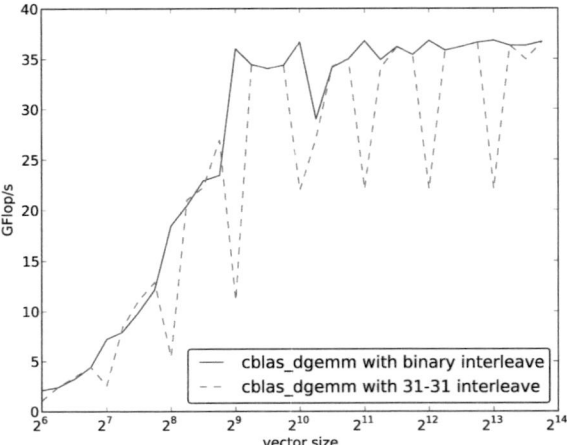

Fig. 8. Performance of the cblas_dgemm matrix-matrix multiplication provided by the CML with 31-31 and binary interleave

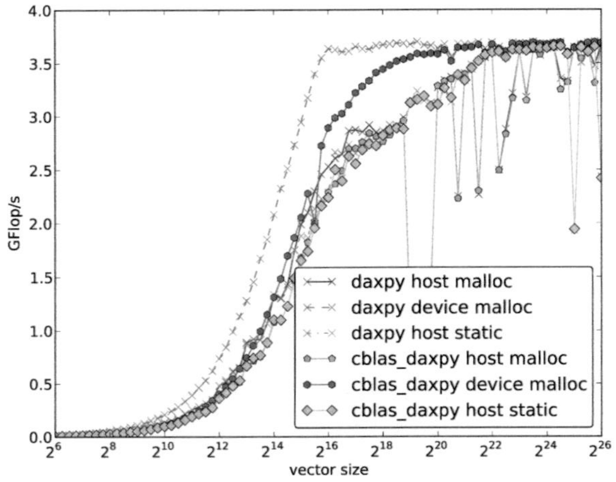

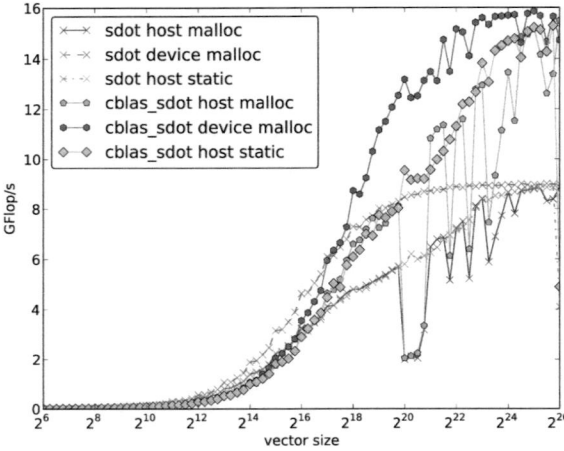

Fig. 10. DAXPY vector update using different implementations and different memory allocation strategies

lengths, allocating and freeing memory on the host and using migration calls in between, the results are even less reliable.

We observe that our own implementations are usually faster for short vector lengths – probably due to lower call overhead and less parameter checking. For longer vector lengths the CML library implementations usually give better results. Results for the SAXPY/DAXPY vector updates are depicted in Figure 9 and in Figure 10. Performance data for the SDOT/DDOT scalar products are shown in Figure 11 and in Figure 12, and for the SGEMV/DGEMV dense matrix-vector multiplication in Figure 13 and in Figure 14.

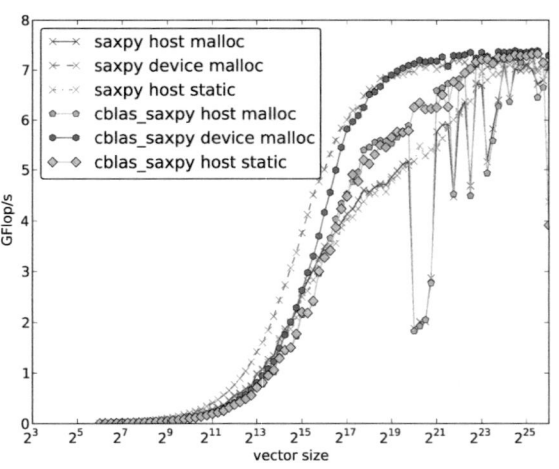

Fig. 9. SAXPY vector update using different implementations and different memory allocation strategies

Fig. 11. SDOT scalar product using different implementations and different memory allocation strategies

E. Sparse Matrix-Vector Multiplication

Many numerical discretization schemes for scientific problems result in sparse system matrices. Typically, iterative methods are used for solving these sparse systems. On top of scalar products and vector updates, the efficiency of sparse matrix-vector multiplications is very important for these scenarios. When using the algorithm for the compressed sparse row (CSR) storage format [11] presented in Figure 15, loops and reduction operations are vectorized by the compiler. However, the performance results are very disappointing – being in the range of a few MFlop/s. Although the memory bandwidth for indexed access as presented in Figure 5 is very good, the relatively short vector length and the overhead of the vector reduction in the inner loop seem to slow down computations

6

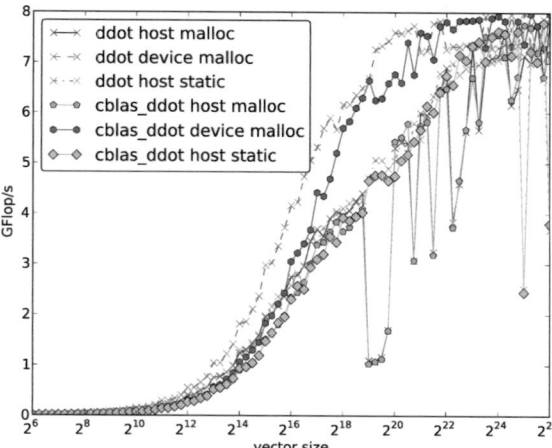

Fig. 12. DDOT scalar product using different implementations and different memory allocation strategies

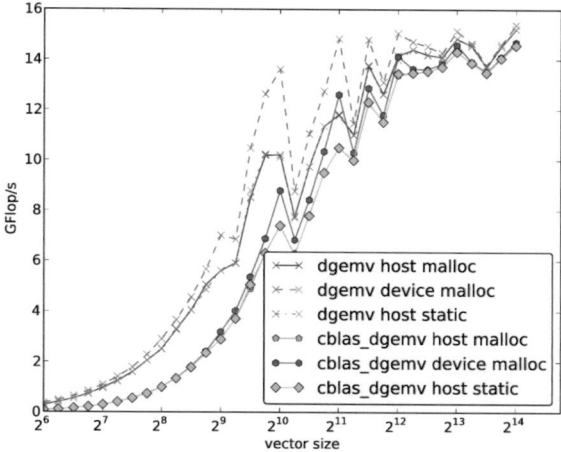

Fig. 14. DGEMV matrix-vector multiplication using different implementations and different memory allocation strategies

```
void spmv(int nrows, float val[],
          int coli[], int rowp[],
          float vin[], float vout[]){
#pragma cny no_loop_dep(val, vin, vout)
#pragma cny no_loop_dep(coli, rowp)
  for( int row = 0; row < nrows; row++ ) {
    int start = rowp[row];
    int end   = rowp[row+1];
    float sum = 0.0;
    for( int i = start; i < end; i++ ) {
      sum += val[i] * vin[coli[i]];
    }
    vout[row] = sum;
  }
}
```

Fig. 15. Sparse matrix-vector multiplication (SpMV) routine for CSR data format

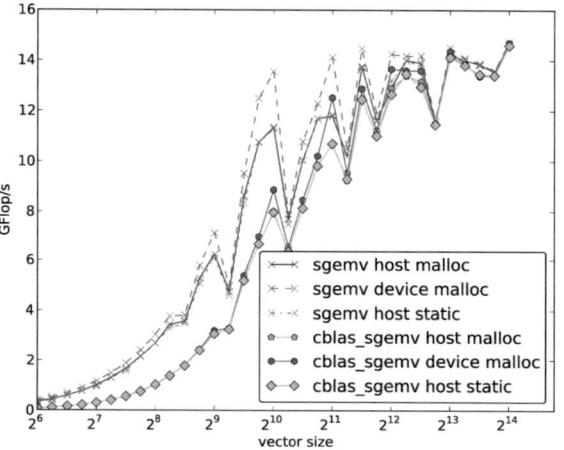

Fig. 13. SGEMV matrix-vector multiplication using different implementations and different memory allocation strategies

(see also observations in Section VI on loop optimizations). Unfortunately, in this case loop reordering is not that easy because the length of the inner loop depends on the outer loop. A possible solution is to use other sparse matrix representations like the ELL format, as used on GPUs e.g. in [12].

F. Stencil Operations

Stencil kernels are one of the most important routines applied in the context of solving partial differential equations (PDEs) on structured grids. They originate from the discretization of differential expressions in PDEs by means of finite element, finite volume or finite difference methods. They are defined as a fixed subset of nearest neighbors where the corresponding node values are used for computing weighted

sums. The associated weights correspond to the coefficients of the PDEs where coefficients are assumed to be constant in our context. In our test we use a 3-dimensional 7-point stencil for solving the Laplace equation on grids of different sizes. The performance results on the HC-1, on an 8-core Nehalem CPU system, and on two different NVIDIA GPUs are shown in Figure 16. Our stencil code for the HC-1 is close to the example given in the Convey documentation material. The CPU implementation is the one used in [13], not using the presented in-place optimization but only conventional space-blocking and streaming optimizations. The NVIDIA CUDA GPU implementation uses blocking of input values in shared memory for data reuse.

For the conventional CPU one can see a high peak for small grid sizes when the data can be kept in the cache. For larger grid sizes a pretty constant performance with slight

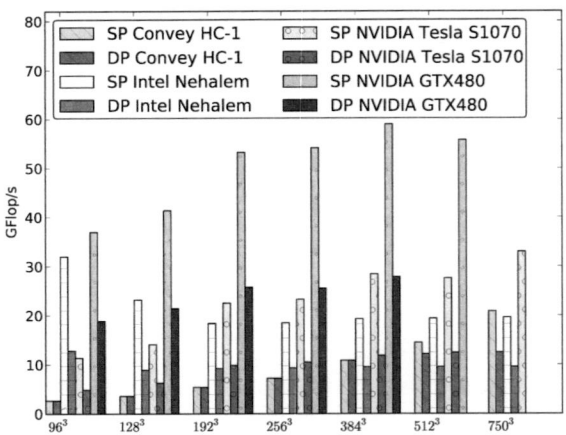

Fig. 16. Performance of a 3-dimensional 7-point Laplace stencil (one grid update is counted as 8 Flop) in single precision (SP) and double precision (DP) on the Convey HC-1, on a 2-way 2.53 GHz Intel Nehalem system using 8 cores, on a single GPU of an NVIDIA Tesla S1070 system, and on an NVIDIA GTX480 consumer GPU

increases due to less loop overhead is observed. The Convey HC-1 on the other hand shows no cache effects but lower performance on smaller grids. But unfortunately because of its lack of caching, neighboring values of the stencil have to be reloaded every time they are needed – wasting a large portion of the much higher total memory bandwidth. On the Convey HC-1 the difference between single and double precision stencil performance becomes apparent only for large grid size. Both NVIDIA GPUs show impressive performance, especially the newer generation. At the same time, they show the restrictive memory limitations – especially for the budget-priced consumer GPU with only 2 GB device memory. Here, the larger samples could not be computed.

VIII. CONCLUSION

Convey's HC-1 Hybrid Core Computer offers seamless integration of a highly capable FPGA platform with an easy coprocessor programming model, a coherent memory space shared by the host and the accelerator, and remarkable bandwidth values on the coprocessor. Moreover, Convey's scatter-gather memory configuration offers advantages for codes with irregular memory access patterns. With Convey's personalities the actual hardware configuration can be adapted to, and optimized for specific application needs. With its HC-1 platform, Convey brings FPGAs closer to high performance computing. However, we have failed to port more complex applications originating in numerical simulation due to the failure to obtain acceptable speed for sparse matrix-vector multiplication.

The HC-1 has the potential to be used for general purpose applications. Although the HC-1 falls behind the impressive performance numbers of GPU systems and the latest multicore CPUs, it provides an innovative approach to asymmetric processing, to compiler-based parallelization, and in particular

to portable programming solutions. Only a single code base is necessary for x86-64 and FPGA platforms which facilitates maintainability of complex codes. In contrast to GPUs, memory capacity is not limited by a few GB and FPGAs connected by direct networks come in reach. A great opportunity lies in the possibility to develop custom personalities – if time, knowledge and costs permit.

Convey's approach represents emerging technology with some deficiencies but also with a high level of maturity. Major drawbacks arise from limitations for floating point arithmetics on FPGAs, compiler capabilities for automatic vectorization, and the usage of Intel's obsolete FSB communication infrastructure. In our experience, typical code bases still show room for code and compiler improvements. While major benefits have been reported for specific workloads in bioinformatics, the HC-1 also provides a viable means for floating point-dominated and bandwidth-limited numerical applications. Despite its high acquisition costs, this breakthrough technology needs further attention.

ACKNOWLEDGEMENTS

The Shared Research Group 16-1 received financial support by the Concept for the Future of Karlsruhe Institute of Technology in the framework of the German Excellence Initiative and by the industrial collaboration partner Hewlett-Packard.

REFERENCES

[1] P. J. Ashenden, *The VHDL Cookbook*. Dept. Computer Science, Univ. Adelaide, S. Australia. [Online]. Available: http://tams-www.informatik.uni-hamburg.de/vhdl/doc/cookbook/VHDL-Cookbook.pdf

[2] D. Thomas and P. Moorby, *The Verilog Hardware Description Language*, 2008.

[3] J. M. P. Cardoso, P. C. Diniz, and M. Weinhardt, "Compiling for reconfigurable computing: A survey," *ACM Comput. Surv.*, vol. 42, pp. 13:1–13:65, June 2010. [Online]. Available: http://doi.acm.org/10.1145/1749603.1749604

[4] A. Shan, "Heterogeneous processing: A strategy for augmenting Moore's law," *Linux J.* [Online]. Available: http://www.linuxjournal.com/article8368

[5] T. M. Brewer, "Instruction set innovations for the Convey HC-1 Computer," *IEEE Micro*, vol. 30, pp. 70–79, 2010.

[6] O. Storaasli and D. Strenski, "Cray XD1 – exceeding 100x speedup/FPGA: Timing analysis yields further gains," in *Proc. 2009 Cray User Group, Atlanta GA*, 2009.

[7] J. Bakos, "High-performance heterogeneous computing with the Convey HC-1," *Computing in Science Engineering*, vol. 12, no. 6, pp. 80 –87, 2010.

[8] J. M. Kunkel and P. Nerge, "System performance comparison of stencil operations with the Convey HC-1," Research Group Scientific Computing, University of Hamburg, Tech. Rep. 2010-11-16, 2010.

[9] Convey Computer, http://www.conveycomputer.com/resources/ConveyBioinformatics_web.pdf.

[10] Basic Linear Algebra Subprograms (BLAS), http://www.netlib.org/blas/.

[11] S. Williams, R. Vuduc, L. Oliker, J. Shalf, K. Yelick, and J. Demmel, "Optimizing sparse matrix-vector multiply on emerging multicore platforms," *Parallel Computing (ParCo)*, vol. 35, no. 3, pp. 178–194, March 2009.

[12] N. Bell and M. Garland, "Efficient sparse matrix-vector multiplication on CUDA," NVIDIA Corporation, NVIDIA Technical Report NVR-2008-004, Dec. 2008.

[13] W. Augustin, V. Heuveline, and J.-P. Weiss, "Optimized stencil computation using in-place calculation on modern multicore systems," pp. 772–784, 2009.

8

Optimized Replacement in the Configuration Layers of the Grid ALU Processor

Ralf Jahr, Basher Shehan, Theo Ungerer
University of Augsburg
Institute of Computer Science
86135 Augsburg, Germany
Email: {jahr, shehan, ungerer}@informatik.uni-augsburg.de

Sascha Uhrig
Technical University Dortmund
Robotics Research Institute
44221 Dortmund, Germany
Email: sascha.uhrig@tu-dortmund.de

Abstract—The Grid ALU Processor comprises a reconfigurable two-dimensional array of ALUs. A conventional sequential instruction stream is mapped dynamically to this array by a special configuration unit within the front-end of the processor pipeline. One of the features of the Grid ALU Processor are its configuration layers, which work like a trace cache to store instruction sequences that have been already mapped to the ALU array recently.

Originally, the least recently used (LRU) strategy has been implemented to evict older configurations from the layers. As we show in this paper the working set is frequently larger than the available number of configuration layers in the processor resulting in thrashing. Hence, there is quite a large gap between the hit rate achieved by LRU and the hit rate achievable with an optimal algorithm. We propose an approach called qdLRU to enhance the performance of the configuration layers. Using qdLRU closes the gap between LRU and an optimal eviction strategy by 66% on average and achieves a maximum performance improvement of 390% and 5.06% on average with respect to the executed instructions per clock cycle (IPC).

Index Terms—Trace Cache, Replacement Strategy, Post-link Optimization, Feedback-directed Optimization, Coarse-Grained Reconfigurable Architecture

I. INTRODUCTION

Within this paper, we present an optimization for the Grid ALU Processor (GAP), which has been introduced by Uhrig et al. [1]. It brings together a superscalar-like processor front-end and a coarse-grained reconfigurable architecture, i.e. a reconfigurable array of functional units (FUs). The front-end consisting of instruction fetch and decode unit is extended with a new configuration unit. This unit maps the instructions from the instruction stream dynamically and at run-time onto the array of FUs. Mapping of instructions and execution of instructions in the array run in parallel until there is a reason to flush the array and restart the mapping process. The mapping which has been built until this moment is called a configuration.

These configurations can be buffered in so-called configuration layers, which are formed by some memory cells very close to all the FUs. The configuration layers are very similar to trace caches. If a part of a program, i.e. a configuration, is already stored in the configuration layers it can be executed faster because it does not have to go through the front-end first, so instruction cache misses cannot occur. The timing inside the

array is optimized, too. Because of this, it is a worthwhile goal to increase the usage of the configuration layers. Analyzing the execution of benchmarks we came to the conclusion that for some of them our default replacement strategy LRU works unexpectedly bad, even worse than replacing a random configuration layer (we call this strategy RANDOM). So LRU is in some cases not clever at all and humbles the execution speed.

The main contributions of this paper are (1) the analysis and comparison of the behavior of well-known replacement algorithms when applied to the replacement in the configuration layers and (2) the introduction and analysis of qdLRU. QdLRU improves the hit rate of LRU by adding flags to the program code based on a feedback-directed approximation of the working sets.

After giving a short introduction of the target platform in Section II, we discuss some basics about replacement strategies in Section III. The extended version of LRU called qdLRU is introduced in Section IV and evaluated in Section V. Related work is presented in Section VI and Section VII concludes the paper.

II. TARGET PLATFORM: THE GRID ALU PROCESSOR

The Grid ALU Processor (GAP) has been developed to speed up the execution of conventional single-threaded instruction streams. To achieve this goal, it combines the advantages of superscalar processor architectures, those of coarse-grained reconfigurable systems, and asynchronous execution.

A superscalar-like processor front-end consisting of fetch- and decode units is used together with a novel configuration unit (see Figure 1(a)) to load instructions and map them dynamically onto an array of functional units (FUs) accompanied by a branch control unit and several load/store units to handle memory accesses (see Figure 1(b)).

The array of FUs is organized in columns and rows. Each column is dynamically and per configuration assigned to one architectural registers. Instructions are assigned to the columns whose register match the instructions' output registers. The rows of the array are used to model dependencies between instructions. If an instruction B is dependent of an instruction A, it will be mapped to a row below the row of A. This way it is possible for the in-order configuration unit to also "issue"

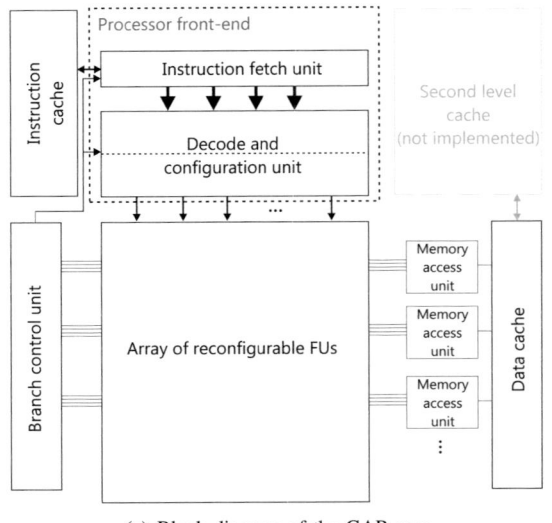

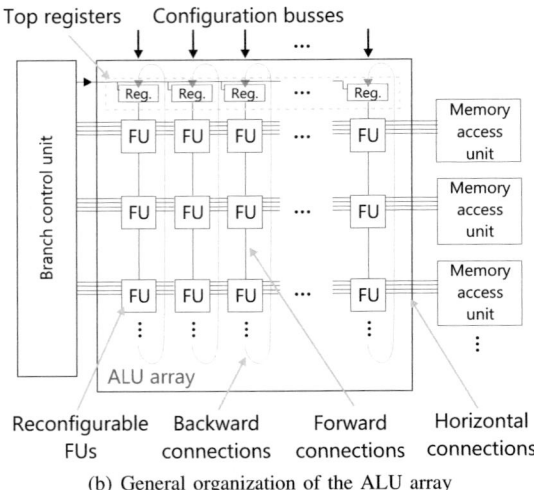

| (a) Block diagram of the GAP core | (b) General organization of the ALU array |

Fig. 1.   Architecture of the Grid ALU Processor

dependent instructions without the need of complex out-of-order logic. A bimodal branch predictor is used to effectively map control dependencies onto the array.

Execution starts in the first row of the array. The dataflow is performed asynchronously inside the array of FUs and it is synchronized with the clock of the branch control unit and the L/S units by so-called timing tokens [1].

Whenever either a branch is miss-predicted or execution reaches the last row of the array with configured FUs the array is cleared and the configuration unit maps new instructions starting from the first row of the array. In order to save configurations for repeated execution all elements of the array are equipped with some memory cells which form configuration layers. Typically, 2, 4, 8, 16, 32, or 64 configuration layers are available. The array is quasi three-dimensional and its size can be written as `columns x rows x layers`.

With this extension it has to be checked before mapping new instructions if the next instruction to execute is equal to the first instruction in any of the layers. If a match is found, the corresponding layer is set to active and execution continues there. If no match is found, the least recently used configuration layer is cleared and used to store the new configuration. In all cases, the new values of registers calculated in columns are copied into the registers at the top of the columns.

To evaluate the architecture a cycle- and signal-accurate simulator has been developed. It uses the Portable Instruction Set Architecture (PISA), hence the simulator can execute the identical program files as the SimpleScalar simulation tool set [2] (but it is not based on it). Detailed information about the processor are given by Uhrig et al. [1] and Shehan et al. [3].

III. TOWARDS AN IMPROVED POLICY

Several basic terms of replacement strategies with respect to the GAP architecture are discussed in this section.

A. Measuring the Performance of a Replacement Strategy

To analyze the performance of a replacement policy, we suggest two measures. The total hit rate h_{total} of the layer subsystem, which is the number of accesses of layers which can be found in the configuration layers a_{hit} divided by the total number of accesses a_{total}. The total hit rate h_{total} can also be understood as the sum of the hit rate by re-accessing the identical configuration subsequently $h_{loop} = a_{loop}/a_{total}$, which is independent from the number of layers available, and the hit rate contributed by the layer subsystem $h_{layer} = a_{layer}/a_{total}$ for all other accesses:

$$h_{total} = \frac{a_{hit}}{a_{total}} = \frac{a_{loop}}{a_{total}} + \frac{a_{layer}}{a_{total}} = h_{loop} + h_{layer}$$

A replacement policy can influence only the hit rate of the layer subsystem h_{layer}. For a given benchmark, h_{loop} has the same value for all replacement strategies.

An optimal offline replacement algorithm (named OPT in the remainder) has been introduced by Belady [4] and it can be used as upper bound. In other words, no (online) replacement policy can achieve a better hit rate than this offline policy, which chooses the element for eviction that will be reused as the last one of all elements in the future.

Another offline algorithm has been mentioned by Temam [5] with the goal to maximize the number of instructions which can be accessed without cache misses. As upper bound for the performance of a replacement policy the algorithm OPT is a much more feasible measure because in the GAP, the penalty caused by activating the front-end of the processor when a new configuration must be build is much higher compared to the time, which is saved when some additional instructions can be found in a layer.

The second measure to evaluate a replacement policy is the performance of the whole system, which is e.g. described by the number of instructions executed per clock cycle (IPC).

B. Known algorithms and their performance

Figure 2 shows the simulated average total hit rate h_{total} of different well-known page replacement policies and the optimal offline policy OPT for 15 benchmarks of the MiBench Benchmark Suite [6] executed on the GAP with an array of width 12 and height 12 and a varying number of configuration layers. The hit rate achieved with one layer is equal to h_{loop} and replacement policies do not have any influence on it. The additional hit rate achieved with more than one layer is contributed by the layer subsystem, i.e. h_{layer}. As expected, LRU performs slightly better than FIFO. The out-performance of RANDOM over LRU is surprising as this replacement strategy behaves quite dumb by evicting random elements.

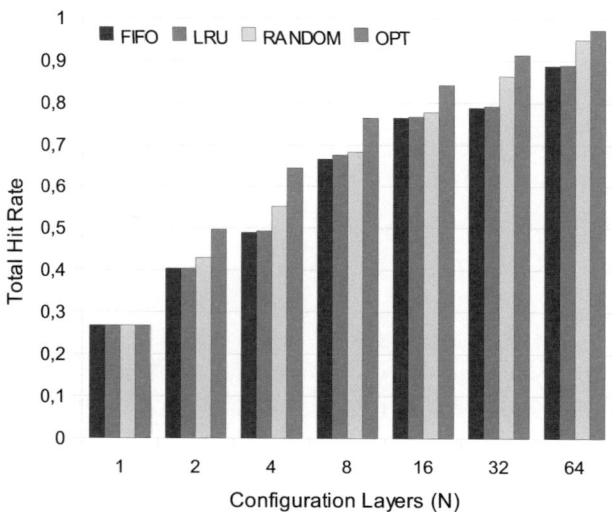

Fig. 2. Average total hit rate over 15 benchmarks for several numbers of configuration layers of GAP configured with an array of 12x12xN functional units

A more detailed view on the hit rate achieved with FIFO, LRU, RANDOM and OPT for the 15 benchmarks on GAP with a 12x12x16 array is presented in Figure 3. Six benchmarks reach a nearly optimal total hit rate close to 1.0 while benchmarks like `auto-qsort`, `netw-dijkstra`, `offi-stringsearch`, `secu-rijndael-encode` and others show a larger gap between the policies.

Table I shows the gap Δ between the performance of LRU and OPT. The second column is the difference Δ of the hit rates of LRU and OPT. In the third column, the achievable improvement with respect to the hit rate of LRU is shown. Closing this gap is the goal of our work.

C. Thrashing as major drawback of LRU

As first step towards an improved replacement policy we designed a graphical representation showing configuration layer accesses and the state of the layers. This type of graphics is referred to as *access plot* in the following. As example, the first 1000 accesses in the layer subsystem are shown in Figure 4(a) and 4(b). To render an access plot, the accesses to configurations are recorded in the GAP simulator. Next,

TABLE I
DIFFERENCE OF THE HIT RATE BETWEEN LRU AND OPT

Layers	Δ	Δ / LRU
1	0	0%
2	0.09	23%
4	0.15	31%
8	0.09	13%
16	0.08	10%
32	0.12	16%
64	0.08	9%
AVG	0.09	15%

each configuration is given an incrementing number (ID). Each access to a configuration is numbered, too. To plot an access, its coordinates are determined by its access number (X-axis) and the number of the accessed configuration (ID, Y-axis). If an already available configuration is accessed, it is colored green (or dark grey, if printed black/white only). If the configuration is not available it is colored red (or black, if printed black/white only). If the target configuration is the same as the one requested by the last access, the current configuration will not be modified. The reuse of the current configuration is not shown in the image because it has no interference with the replacement policy. The content of the layers at the time an access is done is displayed by vertical light gray pixels.

Although only a short part of the total program execution time is visible in Figure III-C it is sufficient to show some important facts. First, there is only a small number of different array configurations compared to the number of actually executed configurations which can be recognized by the width/hight relationship of the plot. Second, several patterns appear very often. They differ mostly by the number of configurations which they contain and the locality [7] of the accesses of the configurations:

- Sequentially executed code, e.g. the starting sequence: The reuse distance is extremely high or unlimited.
- Small loops, i.e. a small number of repeatedly executed configurations: The reuse distance is comparable to the number of configurations of the loop; the number of configurations is smaller than the number of configuration layers.
- Large loops, i.e. a larger number of repeatedly executed configurations: The reuse distance is comparable to the number of configurations of the loop; the number of configurations is larger than the number of configuration layers.
- Program phases: They consist of multiple loops and phases of sequentially executed code. As they contain lots of configurations the locality is only medium. The reuse distance can vary.

In a more detailed analysis we came to the conclusion that the well-known and already mentioned eviction polices show for these patterns always a very similar behavior. For sequential code, none of the strategies can achieve hits because configurations with infinite (or very long) time since a last usage are loaded. Small loops can be handled very well

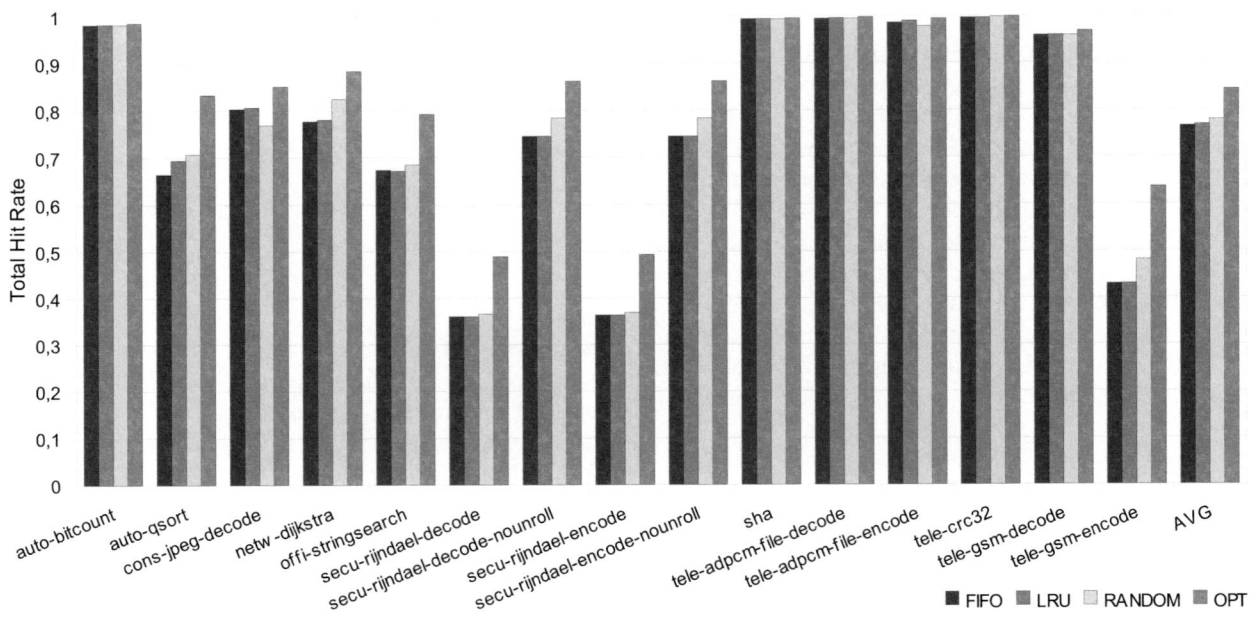

Fig. 3. Total hit rate for the benchmarks run on GAP with a 12x12x16 array

by LRU and OPT. RANDOM does not perform competitive because it evicts random configurations that might be needed again very soon. Large loops are the sticking point. If LRU is used, thrashing (see. e. g. [8]) can occur because the algorithm has to evict configurations that are part of the beginning of the loop and will be reused soon. The hit rate drops to zero. RANDOM performs better because it keeps at least some of the configurations of the loop in the layers. The OPT algorithm does the following: In every iteration of the loop it does not throw away some of the configurations, but keeps them for the next iteration. In Figure 5 the access plots for LRU, RANDOM and OPT can be seen. LRU produces only misses while RANDOM provides some and OPT a reasonable number of hits.

In short, for the replacement of the configuration layers thrashing is the main issue on the way to close the gap between LRU and OPT. Increasing the number of configuration layers would solve this problem to some extend but the number of layers is restricted by their hardware complexity and more complex applications would tend to thrashing again. Therefore, we look for a better replacement strategy to prevent thrashing or at least limit its effects.

IV. QDLRU STRATEGY

The main idea of this new approach is to explicitly add flags to those configurations which would cause thrashing. Those marked configurations are then immediately replaced by another configuration. In other words, they are inserted at the least recently used position instead of the most recently used position. Because the marked configurations are dropped quickly we call the strategy *quick drop LRU* (qdLRU).

As example assume the configurations c_0 to c_{47} are in a working set $W := [c_0, ..., c_{47}]$ and GAP has 32 configuration layers. Repeated executions of W would cause thrashing (when using LRU as replacement strategy) because the size of the working set $|W| = 48$ is larger than 32 which is the number of layers available in the GAP. If W is executed for a longer time with LRU then h_{layer} drops to 0 because of thrashing. The optimal offline strategy would buffer 31 of the 48 configurations, hence: $h_{layer} \approx 31/48 = 0.64583$. With qdLRU you get the same and optimal hit rate for this thrashing-risky situation.

A. Adding flags to instructions

QdLRU is a feedback-directed optimization. The basis to be able to calculate which instructions shall be marked is a trace of addresses of the first instructions of the configurations executed during a program execution. To get this trace file we use the cycle-accurate simulator available for the GAP.

The next step is to find the so-called configuration lines. A configuration line C, e.g. $C = \{c_0, ..., c_{47}\}$, represents one of the diagonal lines in Figure 5 and is very similar to a working set. To generate the set of all configuration lines $\mathbb{C} = \{C_0, ..., C_j\}$ and their usage counters the heuristics described in Listing 1 is used.

These configuration lines represent the working sets with the "smallest degree of reuse". To construct them, we assume that, whenever a configuration is already available in the working set and different from the last handled configuration, a branch back to the start of the current working set is performed.

Afterwards, several configurations within each configuration line are selected as candidates to be dropped quickly. For this, the configuration lines are split into two groups, one group $\mathbb{C}_{short}$ contains all lines whose length is smaller than the

Listing 1. Algorithm to configuration lines

```
input: list<configuration> trace

#define line list<configuration>
set<line> all_lines
map<line, int> line_counters

line current_line = {}
configuration last_configuration

foreach(configuration item in trace)
    if(item == last_configuration)
        // Do nothing
    else if(item ∉ current_line)
        current_line += item
        last_configuration = item
    else
        all_lines += current_line
        line_counters[current_line]++
        current_line = {}
        last_configuration = item
```

number of layers in the processor and the other group $\mathbb{C}_{long}$ contains all the other configuration lines, those configuration lines are too long to fit into the layers without evictions. With having prepared these groups the following algorithm is performed:

1) Select a configuration line `item` from $\mathbb{C}_{long}$.
2) Select from `item` the configuration with the least usage in $\mathbb{C}_{short}$, mark its first instruction.
3) Select all configuration lines from $\mathbb{C}_{long}$ where the number of all configurations minus the number of all marked configurations in the line is smaller than the number of layers of the processor. Move them to $\mathbb{C}_{short}$.
4) If $\mathbb{C}_{long}$ is not empty, restart the algorithm with step 1.

By this heuristic, we select configurations in a manner that they influence as little as possible the execution of configuration lines that fit into the layers. If a configuration line fits into the layers, but one of its configurations is marked, than this can humble the hit rate of this configuration line extremely.

In the last step, our post-link optimization tool GAPtimize (introduced in [9]) is used to mark the first instruction of the selected configurations with a special *drop quickly* flag. This flag directs the configuration layer subsystem of GAP to drop the configuration starting with the actual instruction quickly.

B. Executing the modified binary

When implementing qdLRU, changes are necessary both in hardware and in software. The changes in hardware are very simple. All which has to be done is to make sure that either a configuration beginning with a marked instruction is inserted in the least recently used position in the LRU access queue or that, when looking for a layer for eviction, it is first looked for a configuration layer starting with a marked instruction and then replacing this layer.

If a program is executed on the GAP which has not been optimized (and is hence without flags), then qdLRU behaves exactly like LRU, which still offers reasonable performance. This graceful degradation is one of the requirements of all techniques used for the GAP.

V. EVALUATION

For the practical evaluation we rely on the cycle-accurate simulator which has been developed for the GAP and was extended to support qdLRU. As the hardware complexity of GAP can vary very much because of different sizes of its ALU array, we set it to a fixed size of 12 columns and 12

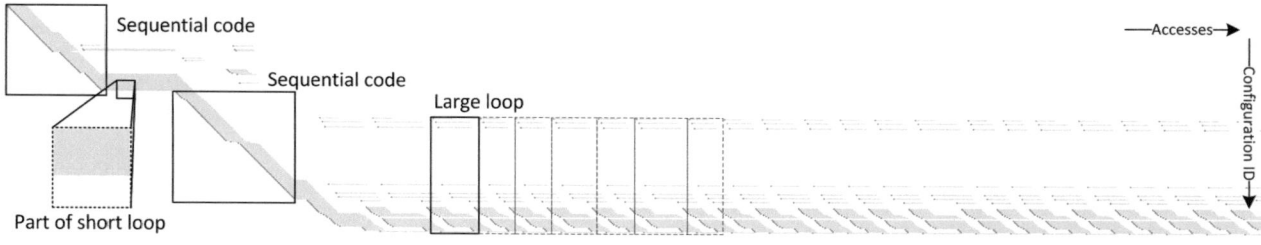

(a) Access plot for the first 1000 accesses of configuration layers for benchmark stringsearch

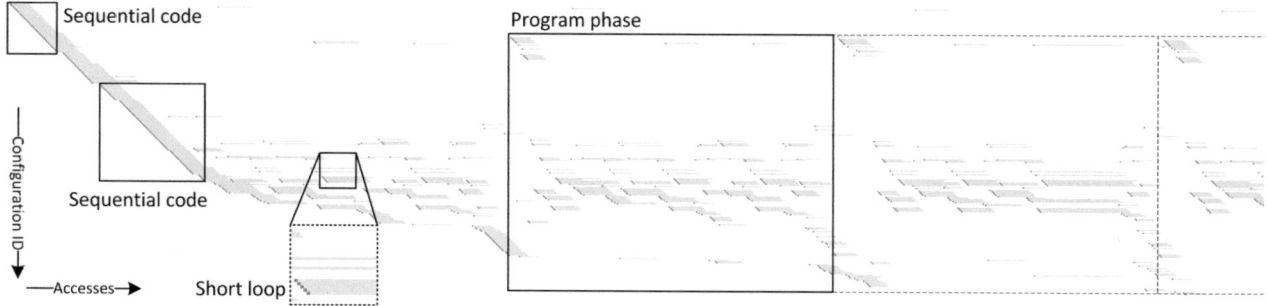

(b) Access plot for the first 1000 accesses of configuration layers for benchmark qsort

Fig. 4. Access plots (see Section III-C) for GAP with 12x12x16 array and LRU as replacement policy; some patterns are marked and labeled.

13

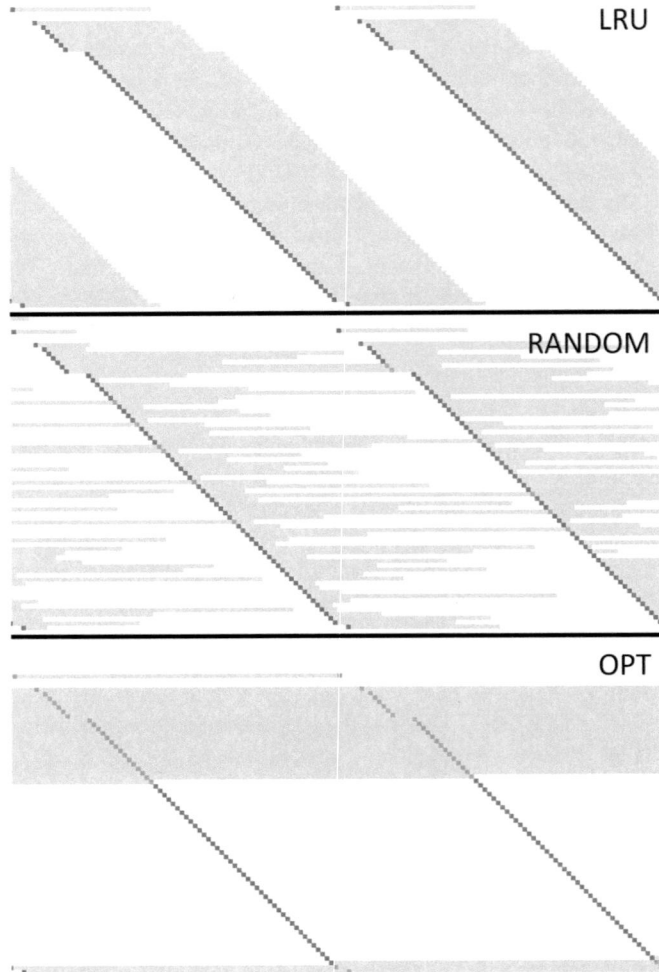

LRU

RANDOM

OPT

Fig. 5. Access plots (see Section III-C) for LRU, RANDOM and OPT (from top to bottom) dealing with a large loop (rijndael on GAP with 12x12x32 array)

rows, which is a realistic size. The performance of the qdLRU policy was evaluated using a varying number of layers. The configuration of the GAP is in the following abbreviated as `columns x rows x layers`.

We use integer-focused benchmarks from the MiBench benchmark suite [6] which have been compiled with GCC for the PISA instruction set architecture (see [2]) with optimizations turned on, i.e. `-O3`. These benchmarks are analyzed and modified with GAPtimize, our tool for feedback-directed post-link optimizations.

For 15 benchmarks, including benchmarks where we expected only little or no change, we achieve an improvement in performance measured by the IPC of 5.06% on average for qdLRU compared to LRU. The highest improvements are achieved for 32 and 64 layers, where we get improvements of 9.48% and 9.41% respectively (compare Figure 8). These values do not seem to be very brilliant which is mainly caused by the fact that for most of the benchmarks we cannot expect the improvement to be very high due to a very small gap

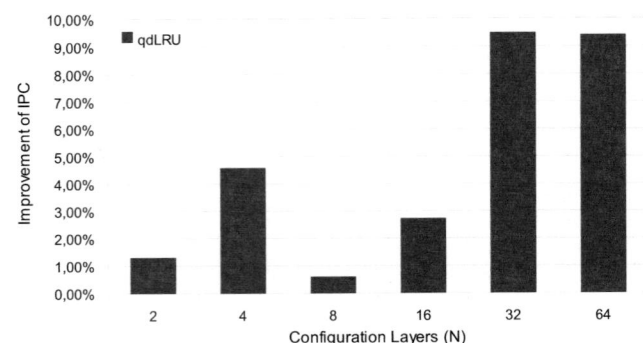

Fig. 6. Average IPC improvement for 15 benchmarks executed on GAP and configurations 12x12xN with qdLRU compared to LRU

between LRU and OPT. Details are shown in Figure 6.

In the top part of Figure 7, more details on the IPC are displayed for some selected benchmarks where thrashing is an issue. The most impressive numbers can be seen for the benchmarks secu-rijndael-decode and secu-rijndael-encode with a maximum improvement of 390 % for the IPC achieved with qdLRU compared to LRU.

This improvement of the IPC is mainly based on the improved hit rate of the layer subsystem. The total average improvement of the hit rate over 15 benchmarks and all configurations is 0.06. This average hit-rate improvement seems to be small but it has to seen in relation to the maximal possible improvement (0.09) which can be achieved with the optimal algorithm OPT (see Section III-B).

For selected benchmarks which might cause thrashing with LRU the total hit rate can be seen in the bottom part of Figure 7. Here again, the benchmarks secu-rijndael-encode and secu-rijndael-decode show supreme results as thrashing is here a very critical problem when using LRU.

In Figure 8 we show the average performance of LRU and qdLRU compared to OPT and RANDOM. QdLRU shows better performance than LRU and RANDOM. The gap between LRU and OPT can be closed with qdLRU by 65.97 % on average, varying between 48,38 % for 2 layers and 78,05% for 32 layers (see Figure 9).

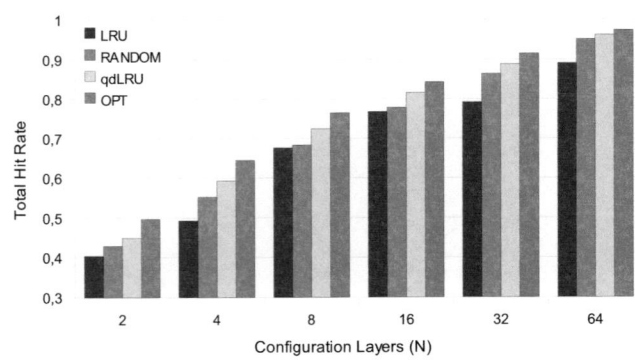

Fig. 8. Simulated total hit rate for LRU, RANDOM, qdLRU and OPT (average over 15 benchmarks, GAP with 12x12xN functional units)

14

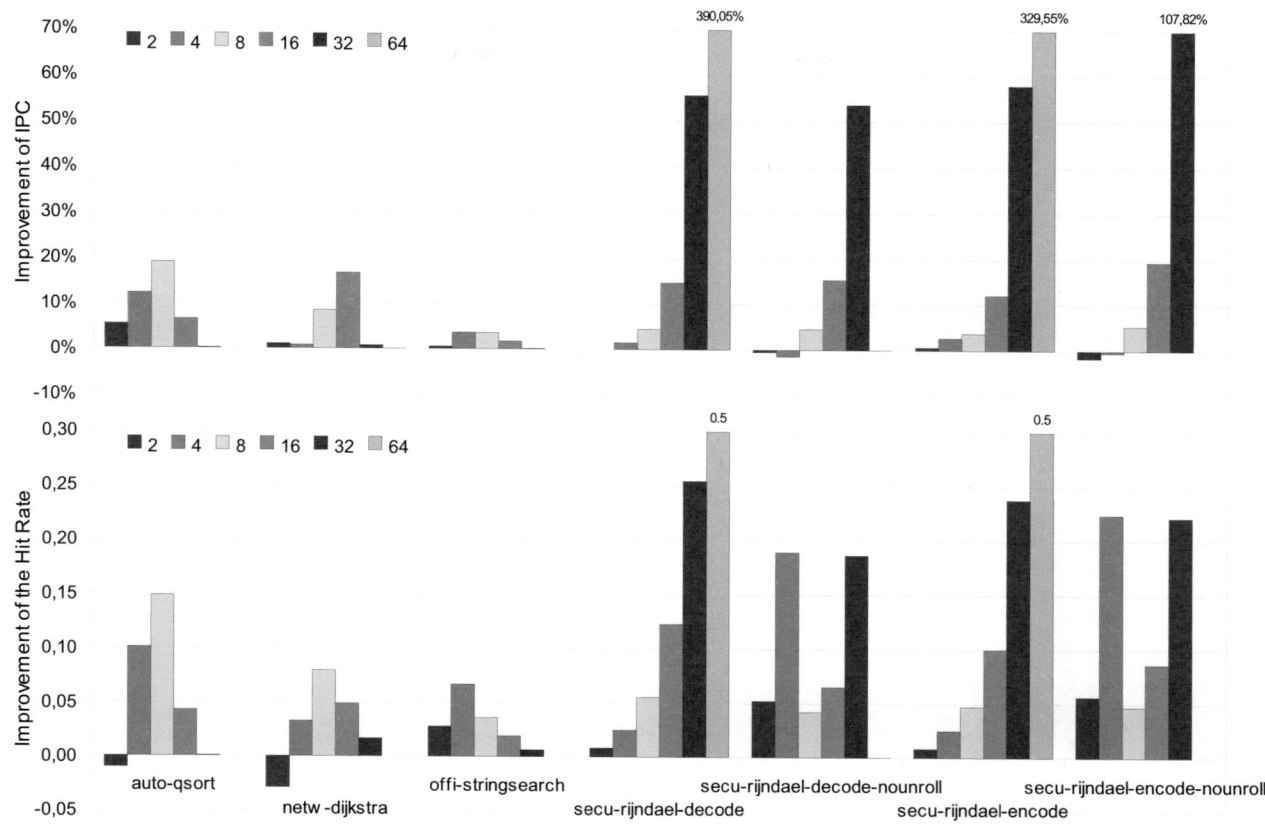

Fig. 7. Relative improvement of the IPC (top) and improvement of the hit rate (bottom) for selected thrashing-risky benchmarks run on GAP with configurations 12x12xN for qdLRU compared to LRU

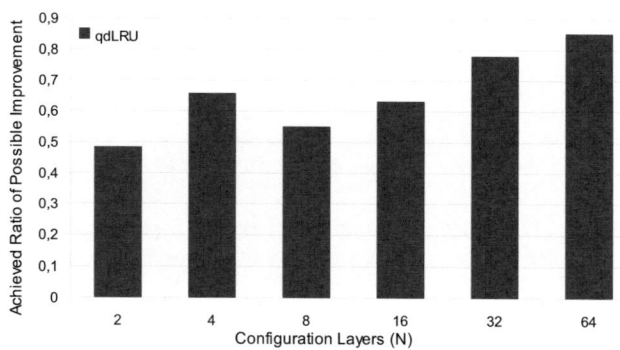

Fig. 9. Ratio of the gap between qdLRU an OPT which can be covered by qdLRU (average over 15 benchmarks, GAP with 12x12xN functional units)

If the memory latency (which has been set to 24 clock cycles) is increased, we expect the effect of an improved hit rate to have stronger implications on the system performance. On the other side, if the size of the also available instruction cache is increased, the effect of increasing the hit rate will decrease because the penalty to load instructions from the instruction cache will decrease due to less instruction cache misses.

VI. RELATED WORK

As mentioned before the configuration layers of the GAP are used to buffer configurations. They work like a cache and a replacement policy is implemented to find the element to evict if space is needed to load a new one. For the GAP, finding a suitable replacement strategy for the configuration layers has not yet been explored. Nevertheless, related work can be found mainly dealing with caches in general and trace caches.

The main difference of the replacement problem for configuration layers compared to general caches is the extremely small number of configurations layers compared to the large number of lines in caches. Because of this, thrashing-risky situations where the working set is larger than the number of available lines are much more frequent for configuration layers than for caches.

Our goal is to find a lightweight solution which can make use of the software infrastructure already available and used for other platform-specific code optimizations, e.g. static speculation [9]. Because of this, our attention is drawn to techniques using both hardware- and software techniques.

As hardware-only solutions, two classes of strategies are known. The first are well-known algorithms which can be implemented with small or reasonable effort in hardware. Some of those strategies are FIFO, RANDOM, WsClock [10] and LRU. From these strategies, LRU is deemed to be the superior one. Together with OPT as upper bound the performance of LRU, FIFO and RANDOM have been compared for our situation in Section III-B.

The second class of algorithms are the Dynamic Insertion Policy (DIP) proposed by Qureshi et al. [11] and the Shepherd Cache proposed by Rajan etc al. [12]. Both share the property that they require additional hardware effort. In our experiments, we also got for our particular situation performance numbers at most comparable to LRU for the Shepherd Cache. The DIP is only applicable if it can select between LRU and BIP with extreme parameters to prevent thrashing. The suggested approach to divide the configuration layers into two sets does not seem to be applicable due to the small number of configuration layers. The small number of lines prevents using strategies like ARC [13] where the lines are split into two sections and handled in different ways.

Some other techniques have also been proposed (see e.g. [14]) but most of them either require large changes of the hardware and/or are not supposed to work well because the low number of layers available in the GAP normally restricts the eventual gain in performance caused by replacement strategies.

Trace caches as introduced by Rotenberg et al. [15] work for superscalar processors very similar to the configuration layers because they are used to buffer parts of a program flow, too. To our knowledge, nobody has yet been working on thrashing situations in this context.

VII. CONCLUSION AND FUTURE WORK

We introduced a software-supported replacement strategy for the configuration layers of the GAP processor, which are used like a trace cache to buffer instructions sequences ready for execution. So far, LRU is used as replacement strategy which offers an unsatisfying performance for several benchmarks. Strangely enough, LRU shows for some benchmarks even worse performance than RANDOM, a strategy evicting a random element. The main reason for this is thrashing, which can happen if the elements of a working set are processed repeatedly and sequentially, i.e. there is a huge degree of locality, and the set contains more configurations than the GAP provides configuration layers. In this case, the hit rate achieved with LRU collapses.

To overcome this issue, we proposed a replacement strategy called qdLRU and a heuristic to approximate the working sets in software. Based on working sets we select some configurations which are evicted immediately from the configuration layers. With this, we can draw the behavior of qdLRU nearer to the optimal strategy OPT. The performance measured by the IPC for qdLRU is on average 5.06% higher than the performance achieved by LRU. A peak improvement of 390% is gained for secu-rinjdael-decode caused by a peak improvement of the hit rate of 0.5.

This approach could be adapted for all situations in which a replacement strategy is needed for a small number of complex elements with many thrashing-risky situations. The introduced strategy requires only very little changes of the hardware when LRU has already been implemented. It also supports graceful degradation back to LRU.

As future work, we propose to work on the detection of working sets. The rule which has been introduced is simple and effective. Nevertheless, there are situations where this rule cannot find a sufficient solution. Hence, to find better solutions it should be thought about the scope of the working sets. From our point of view, it is important that the configurations in a working set should be executed repeatedly in the same order. If this restriction is weakened, the scope of working sets could be enlarged which must be handled carefully but might lead to further improved results. Concluding, it might be possible to find better solutions with biologically inspired algorithms, e.g. ant algorithms or genetic algorithms. Linear programming should also be taken into consideration.

REFERENCES

[1] S. Uhrig, B. Shehan, R. Jahr, and T. Ungerer, "The two-dimensional superscalar gap processor architecture," *International Journal on Advances in Systems and Measurements*, 2010.

[2] D. Burger and T. Austin, "The simplescalar tool set, version 2.0," *ACM SIGARCH Computer Architecture News*, vol. 25, no. 3, pp. 13–25, June 1997.

[3] B. Shehan, R. Jahr, S. Uhrig, and T. Ungerer, "Reconfigurable grid alu processor: Optimization and design space exploration," in *Proceedings of the 13th Euromicro Conference on Digital System Design (DSD) 2010, Lille, France*, 2010.

[4] L. A. Belady, "A study of replacement algorithms for a virtual-storage computer," *IBM Systems*, vol. 5, no. 2, pp. 78–101, 1966.

[5] O. Temam, "Investigating optimal local memory performance," *SIGOPS Oper. Syst. Rev.*, vol. 32, no. 5, pp. 218–227, 1998.

[6] M. Guthaus, J. Ringenberg, D. Ernst, T. Austin, T. Mudge, and T. Brown, "MiBench: A free, commercially representative embedded benchmark suite," *4th IEEE International Workshop on Workload Characteristics*, pp. 3–14, December 2001.

[7] P. J. Denning, "The locality principle," *Commun. ACM*, vol. 48, no. 7, pp. 19–24, 2005.

[8] P. Denning, "Thrashing: its causes and prevention," in *AFIPS '68 (Fall, part 1): Proceedings of the December 9-11, 1968, fall joint computer conference, part I*. New York, NY, USA: ACM, 1968, pp. 915–922.

[9] R. Jahr, B. Shehan, S. Uhrig, and T. Ungerer, "Static speculation as post-link optimization for the grid alu processor," in *Proceedings of the 4th Workshop on Highly Parallel Processing on a Chip (HPPC 2010)*, 2010.

[10] R. W. Carr and J. L. Hennessy, "WSCLOCK - a simple and effective algorithm for virtual memory management," in *SOSP '81: Proceedings of the eighth ACM symposium on Operating systems principles*. New York, NY, USA: ACM Press, 1981, pp. 87–95.

[11] M. K. Qureshi, A. Jaleel, Y. N. Patt, S. C. Steely, and J. Emer, "Adaptive insertion policies for high performance caching," in *ISCA '07: Proceedings of the 34th annual international symposium on Computer architecture*. New York, NY, USA: ACM, 2007, pp. 381–391.

[12] K. Rajan and G. Ramaswamy, "Emulating optimal replacement with a shepherd cache," in *MICRO 40: Proceedings of the 40th Annual IEEE/ACM International Symposium on Microarchitecture*. Washington, DC, USA: IEEE Computer Society, 2007, pp. 445–454.

[13] N. Megiddo and D. S. Modha, "Outperforming lru with an adaptive replacement cache algorithm," *Computer*, vol. 37, no. 4, pp. 58–65, 2004.

[14] G. Keramidas, P. Petoumenos, and S. Kaxiras, "Where replacement algorithms fail: a thorough analysis," in *CF '10: Proceedings of the 7th ACM international conference on Computing frontiers*. New York, NY, USA: ACM, 2010, pp. 141–150.

[15] E. Rotenberg, S. Bennett, and J. E. Smith, "Trace cache: a low latency approach to high bandwidth instruction fetching," in *MICRO 29: Proceedings of the 29th annual ACM/IEEE international symposium on Microarchitecture*. Washington, DC, USA: IEEE Computer Society, 1996, pp. 24–35.

Performance Engineering of an Orthogonal Matching Pursuit Algorithm for Sparse Representation of Signals on Different Architectures

Markus Stürmer, Harald Köstler
University of Erlangen-Nuremberg
91058 Erlangen
Germany

Florian Rathgeber
Imperial College London
London SW7 2AZ
United Kingdom

Abstract—**Modern multicore architectures require adapted, parallel algorithms and implementation strategies for many applications. As a non-trivial example we chose in this paper a patch-based sparse coding algorithm called Orthogonal Matching Pursuit (OMP) and discuss parallelization and implementation strategies on current hardware. The OMP algorithm is used in imaging and involves heavy computations on many small blocks of pixels called patches. From a global view the patches within the image can be processed completely in parallel but within one patch the algorithm is hard to parallelize. We compare the performance on the Cell Broadband Engine Architecture (CBEA), different GPUs, and current multicore CPUs.**

Index Terms—**Batch-OMP algorithm, orthogonal matching pursuit, GPGPU, Cell Broadband Engine Architecture, performance engineering, multicore**

I. INTRODUCTION

Since image acquisition systems produce more and more data and most imaging applications are time-critical, efficient implementations are needed that run on current hardware.

In this work we consider sparse coding, i.e. finding sparse representations of signals or images, based on a frame (overcomplete basis), the so-called dictionary. Sparse representations are widely used and currently state-of-the-art in imaging applications like image denoising, super-resolution, or image restoration [1], [2], [3]. Since sparse coding is in general an NP-hard problem, we reduce the complexity for the creation of the sparse representation of an image by decomposing it into many small blocks called patches. Then, sparse coding is done independently for each of them. While the patches thus can be processed completely in parallel, within one patch the very time-consuming and hardly parallelizable task is to find the coefficients for the sparse representation in the given basis. We solve this approximately by a variant of an orthogonal matching pursuit (OMP) [4], the Batch-OMP algorithm [5].

In previous work we have shown that sparse representations are suitable for CT image denoising and compared the results to other denoising approaches [6], [7], [8], [9]. We also accelerated the Batch-OMP algorithm on the Cell Broadband Engine Architecture (CBEA) in order to achieve close to real-time performance [10]. In this paper we compare the performance of the Batch-OMP algorithm on different hardware architectures like standard CPUs, the CBEA, and GPUs.

Sparse coding is a prominent topic and thus several other contributions have been made by other groups. GPU, CPU, and CBEA implementations for the related compressive sensing are presented in [11], [12] and general image reconstruction algorithms on GPUs in [13]. In [14], a matching pursuit algorithm is implemented on the GPU, which is easier to parallelize and requires less computational effort than OMP. Closest to our work are Septimus and Steinberg [15], who port the Batch-OMP algorithm to a Xilinx Virtex 5 FPGA, and Braun [16], who shows a GPU implementation of the Batch-OMP algorithm. Since Braun states that GPUs are not significantly better or worse than CPUs for OMP, we decided to make a deeper analysis. We achieve better performance with our manually tuned code, but still observe interestingly similar results for CBEA, GPUs and standard CPUs. This is due to the versatile requirements of the different parts of OMP algorithm which cancel out the specifics of each platform.

In the following we give more details about sparse representations and the Batch-OMP algorithm in section II. After that we discuss our GPU implementation strategy in section III and in section IV we present a performance comparison on CPU, GPU, and CBEA. Future work is outlined in section V.

II. METHODS

A. Sparse representation

The goal of a sparse representation of a signal is to reduce the amount of data required to store it. This is achieved by first defining a frame — an overcomplete basis of the signal vector space— that is also called dictionary and then representing signals compactly by a linear combination of only few vectors out of the frame. The signals can also be represented only approximately to reduce data. Mathematically, the problem of finding the sparsest representation $a \in \mathbb{R}^K$ of a signal $X \in \mathbb{R}^n$, up to a given error tolerance $\epsilon > 0$, can be formulated as:

$$\min_{\mathbf{a}} \|\mathbf{a}\|_0 \text{ subject to } \|\mathbf{Da} - \mathbf{X}\|_2 \leq \epsilon , \quad (1)$$

where $\|\cdot\|_0$ denotes the ℓ_0 - seminorm that counts the nonzero entries of a vector $\|\mathbf{a}\|_0 = \sum_{j=0}^{K} |\mathbf{a}_j|^0$. The full rank matrix $\mathbf{D} \in \mathbb{R}^{n \times K}$ is the dictionary that forms an overcomplete basis of the signal space (i.e. $K > n$). Its column vectors are called atoms.

A suitable dictionary, that we use throughout our paper, is a frame derived from cosine functions. An alternative would be dictionary training with the K-SVD algorithm [17].

Unfortunately, exactly determining the sparsest representation of signals is an NP-hard combinatorial problem [4], [18]. Therefore, one usually does not try to find the sparsest representation of the whole signal directly, but one divides $\mathbf{X}$ into small, typically overlapping patches $\mathbf{x}$ and solves (1) for each patch separately in order to reduce the computational effort. The single patches are treated independently of each other and at the end they are assembled to obtain the whole signal $\mathbf{X}$.

B. Orthogonal Matching Pursuit

Orthogonal matching pursuit (OMP) [19], a simple greedy algorithm, solves (1) approximately by sequentially selecting dictionary atoms. OMP is guaranteed to converge in finite-dimensional spaces within a finite number of iterations [4]. The complexity of this algorithm for finding n atoms is $\mathcal{O}(n^3)$ [5]. In each iteration it proceeds as follows:

- First, the projection of the residual $\mathbf{r}$ on the dictionary $\mathbf{p} = \mathbf{D}^T \mathbf{r}$ is computed, and the atom $\hat{k} = \underset{k}{\operatorname{argmax}} |\mathbf{p}|$ with maximal correlation to the residual is selected.
- Then, the current patch $\mathbf{x}$ is orthogonally projected onto the span of the selected atoms by computing $\mathbf{a} = (\mathbf{D}_I)^+ \mathbf{x}$. This orthogonalization step ensures that all selected atoms are linearly independent [5].
- Finally, the new residual is computed by $\mathbf{r} = \mathbf{x} - \mathbf{D}_I \mathbf{a}$, which is orthogonal to all previously selected atoms.

Here, $\mathbf{I}$ denotes a set containing indices of selected atoms, $\mathbf{D}_I$ are the corresponding columns of $\mathbf{D}$ and $(\mathbf{D}_I)^+$ represents the pseudoinverse of $\mathbf{D}_I$.

The Batch-OMP algorithm [5], summarized in algorithm 1, accelerates the OMP algorithm for larger patch sizes. It pre-computes the Gram matrix $\mathbf{G} = \mathbf{D}^T \mathbf{D}$ and the initial projection $\mathbf{p}^0 = \mathbf{D}^T \mathbf{x}$ in order to require only the projection of the residual on the dictionary instead of explicitly computing the residual. In addition to that we replace the computation of the pseudoinverse in the orthogonalization step, which is done in OMP by a singular value decomposition, with a progressive Cholesky update performed in lines 5 - 8 of algorithm 1 by means of forward substitution. The two subscripts at the Gram matrix in line 6 indicate that entries of the Gram matrix in rows corresponding to previously chosen atoms and in the column corresponding to the latest chosen atom are considered. The orthogonalization and residual update step in the OMP algorithm can be written as

$$\mathbf{r} = \mathbf{x} - \mathbf{D}_I (\mathbf{D}_I^T \mathbf{D}_I)^{-1} \mathbf{D}_I^T \mathbf{x} . \quad (2)$$

Due to orthogonalization, the matrix $(\mathbf{D}_I^T \mathbf{D}_I)$ is symmetric positive definite, which allows the Cholesky decomposition. In each iteration, the triangular matrix $\mathbf{L}$ is extended by another row.

Algorithm 1 a = Batch-OMP $\left(\mathbf{p}^0 = \mathbf{D}^T\mathbf{x}, \; \epsilon_0 = \mathbf{x}^T\mathbf{x}, \; \mathbf{G} = \mathbf{D}^T\mathbf{D}\right)$

1 Init: Set $I = \emptyset$, $\mathbf{L}_1 = [1]$, $\mathbf{a} = 0$, $\delta_0 = 0$, $\mathbf{p} = \mathbf{p}^0$, $i = 1$

2 **while** $\epsilon_{i-1} > \epsilon$ **do**

3    $\hat{k} = \underset{k}{\operatorname{argmax}} |\mathbf{p}|$

4    $I_i = I_{i-1} \cup \hat{k}$

5   **if** $i > 1$ **then**

6       $\mathbf{w} = $ Solve: $\mathbf{L}_{i-1}\mathbf{w} = \mathbf{G}_{I_{i-1},\hat{k}}$

7   where $\mathbf{L}_i = \begin{bmatrix} \mathbf{L}_{i-1} & 0 \\ \mathbf{w}^T & \sqrt{1 - \mathbf{w}^T\mathbf{w}} \end{bmatrix}$

8   **end if**

9    $\mathbf{a}_{I_i} = $ Solve: $\mathbf{L}_i \left(\mathbf{L}_i\right)^T \mathbf{a}_{I_i} = \mathbf{p}^0_{I_i}$

10   $\beta = \mathbf{G}_{I_i}\mathbf{a}_{I_i}$

11   $\mathbf{p} = \mathbf{p}^0 - \beta$

12   $\delta_i = \mathbf{a}_{I_i}^T \beta_{I_i}$

13   $\epsilon_i = \epsilon_{i-1} - \delta_i + \delta_{i-1}$

14   $i = i + 1$

15 **end while**

The non-zero element coefficient vector $\mathbf{a}_{I_i}$ is computed in line 9 by means of a forward- and backward substitution. In line 11 we update the projection

$$\mathbf{p} = \mathbf{D}^T\mathbf{r} = \mathbf{p}^0 - \mathbf{G}_I \left(\mathbf{D}_I\right)^+ \mathbf{x} \; . \qquad (3)$$

When an error-constrained sparse approximation problem is to be solved, the residual is required to check the termination criterion. The ℓ_2 norm of the residual ϵ_i is computed in line 13.

III. GPU IMPLEMENTATION

A first approach to port Batch-OMP to CUDA [20] was to perform sparse coding of one patch in a single thread block as a monolithic kernel. Data is held on-chip in registers and shared memory, but the working set is too large to allow for many such blocks to be active concurrently on a given multiprocessor. Furthermore, the degree of parallelism changes strongly during the computation, keeping most threads idle for a large portion of the kernel execution. The results shown in table I confirm the results of [16] that this approach is inferior.

A better solution computes the sparse representation of as many patches as possible concurrently, allowing for at least as many CUDA threads as patches throughout the whole algorithm. Consequently, scalars in algorithm 1 become vectors, and vectors become columns of matrices. However, we still keep the symbols from the algorithm description.

As input, the dictionary $\mathbf{D}$, the Gram matrix $\mathbf{G}$ and a two-dimensional array containing all patches $\mathbf{x}$ are taken. Instead of computing each of them separately, all $\mathbf{p}^0$s can be computed by a matrix-matrix multiplication of the matrix containing all $\mathbf{x}$ (or its transpose, depending on storage scheme) with $\mathbf{D}^T$ using a CUBLAS call. Another kernel computes a vector containing all initial errors e_0.

To find the next atom from the dictionary and the optimal coefficients for the respective set, four kernel calls are required each time:

find next atom: As it is required only for this task, all values of $\mathbf{p} = \mathbf{p}^0 - \beta$ are computed on the fly, which requires to have β initialized as zero. One thread is used for each patch. This task corresponds to lines 3, 4, and 11 of the algorithm.

substitutions: All operations involving L, corresponding to lines 5 to 9, are performed by a single kernel. Values from the Gram matrix are fetched from the texture unit, which performed best also on the Fermi architecture. All temporaries during the substitution are held in shared memory. It should also be mentioned that the forward substitution $\mathbf{L}_i\mathbf{t_i} = \mathbf{p}^0_{I_i}$ in line 9 needs only to compute a single additional element to $\mathbf{t_{i-1}}$. Again, one thread is used per patch.

projection: Line 10 of the algorithm corresponds to a matrix-sparse-vector product for each patch. In contrast to the other kernels, two completely different strategies are used on CUDA compute capability 1.3 and 2.

For 1.3, blocks of 16×16 are used to compute β for 16 patches. First, coefficients and indices are copied to shared memory, with the x-dimension determining the patch. Then threads synchronize, and now the x-dimension determines the elements of β and the y-dimension the patch. The computed elements are stored in shared memory, and only written to device memory after synchronizing again and associating the x-dimension with patches again. As temporary data is stored with an appropriate padding, it is possible to load and store it column- as well as row-wise without bank conflicts in shared memory. The flipping of the orientation further ensures that global and texture memory are accessed contiguously. The code is further unrolled so that four elements of β are computed by a thread at a time.

For the Fermi architecture, which introduces a configurable 16 KiB or 48 KiB L1 and 768 KiB unified L2 cache, the kernel simplifies drastically. All data is fetched from device memory completely relying on the caches. Some blocking is performed by having each thread computing eight elements at a time. The y-dimension of the grid can be used to compute different elements of β concurrently.

error update: Computation of the new error corresponds to lines 12 and 13 of the algorithms. The scattered accesses to β are best treated by mapping the storage to texture memory, but for i being small (typically up to two or three) it is faster to recompute the respective elements of β, as accesses to **G** have a much better cache reuse.

A drawback of this implementation strategy is that for each patch the same number of atoms needs to be chosen. Approaches that allow to continue only with patches that could not yet be represented good enough without drastically losing performance are still being explored.

IV. RESULTS

We measured the performance of our Batch-OMP implementation on an NVIDIA GTX480 GPU and an NVIDIA GTX295 dual-GPU. The former provides 15 multiprocessors (MP) of CUDA compute capability 2.0 that access 1.5 GiB of main memory with a theoretical peak bandwidth of 177.4 GB/s. The latter provides two GPUs, each consisting of 30 MPs of compute capability 1.3, each having access to 896 MiB of device memory with a peak bandwidth of 111.9 GB/s each. The results for the GTX295 have been measured on a single GPU and doubled where appropriate.

We are using our implementation [10] for the Cell Broadband Engine Architecture (CBEA) as comparison. The CBEA results are measured using very precise counters on a single compute core, a so-called synergistic processing element (SPE), and extrapolated to a whole two-socket system. As no double precision is required, the older Cell/B.E. and the newer PowerXCell8i processors perform equally fast for this kernel. The results are therefore equally valid for IBM's QS20, QS21 and QS22 blade servers, whose two CPUs have the same clock frequency of 3.2 GHz and provide 8 SPEs each.

We also compare against an implementation in C99 which has been optimized for performance, but without usage of libraries or compiler intrinsics. Test are run on a Fujitsu Celsius R570 workstation containing two Intel Xeon X5670 processors (Westmere core). Each processor has six cores at a base frequency of 2.93 GHz, but this can increase to 3.33 GHz for a single core using Intel's TurboBoost technology. Each core provides a second virtual core using simultaneous multithreading (SMT).

System performance

Figure 1 shows how many patches can be processed on a whole system depending on the number of atoms to be chosen. Quite surprisingly, both GPUs and the Cell blades are close with a small advantage for the GPUs when only few atoms should be used and for the CBEA for three or more. The x86-64 system is slower especially for few atoms to be chosen due to the scalar matrix multiplications in C99. This is even more surprising when considering that all data for processing a single patch fits into a Xeons core's L2 caches or an SPE's local storage, but that the graphics card must largely operate on device memory due to the high degree of parallelism.

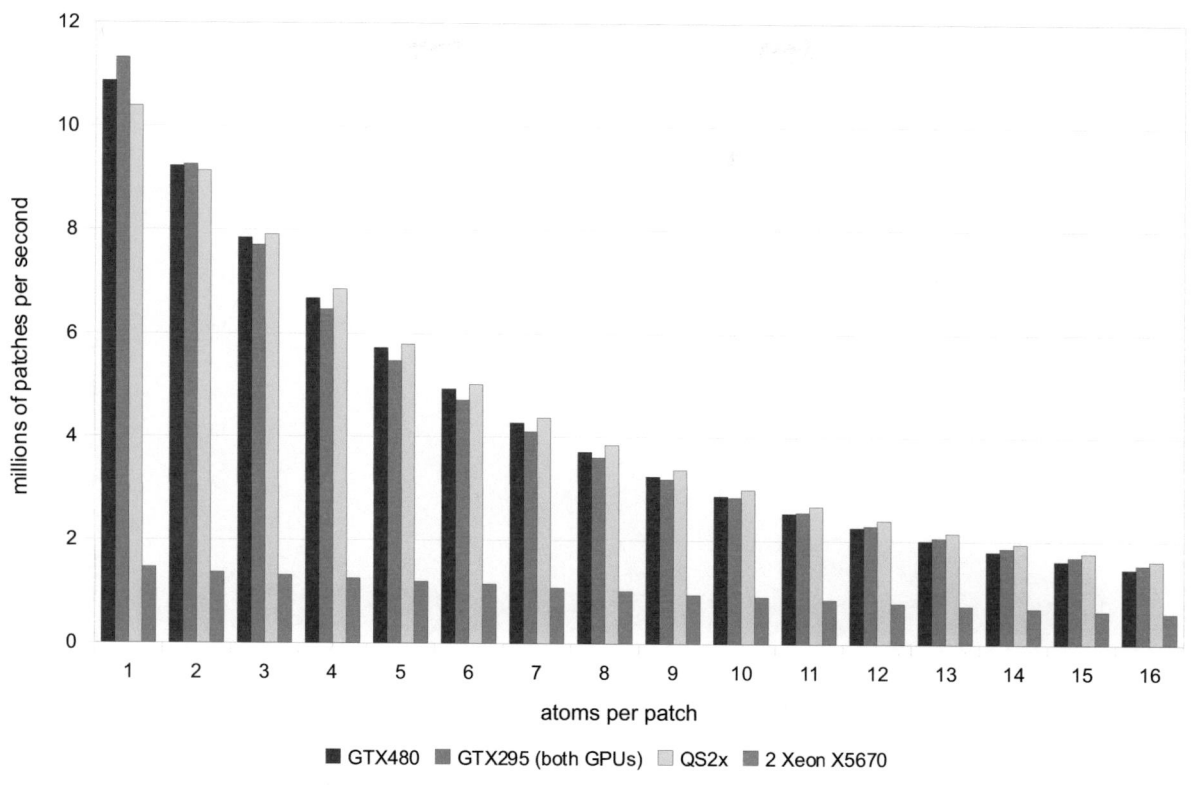

Figure 1.   Patches per second depending on number of atoms to be chosen and test platform.

To eliminate this effect, table I compares the performance of the kernels without this initialization. The workstation now can nearly keep up for few atoms to be chosen. After all, we compare a general high-level language kernel that received hours of optimization to carefully tuned codes that received days. Included are also the results for the first implementation that performs Batch-OMP for a patch in a single thread block, but only one block can be active per MP on the GTX295 at any given time, and five on the GTX480.

Compute unit performance

Another view on performance is shown in figure 2, which compares the performance of one compute unit of the test platforms. It compares how many patches can be processed by a multiprocessor, SPE, or core per second, excluding the initialization. The performance of an MP in the GTX295 is by far the lowest and demonstrates that this dual-GPU maxed out the facilities of the older architecture by combining as many compute cores as possible. An

Table I
MILLIONS OF PATCHES PER SECOND DEPENDING ON NUMBER OF
ATOMS TO BE CHOSEN AND TEST PLATFORM WITHOUT
INITIALIZATION.

	1	2	4	8	16
GTX480	69.68	32.45	13.87	5.21	1.65
GTX295 (both GPUs)	52.63	25.82	11.75	4.81	1.73
QS2x	60.74	33.77	15.17	5.55	1.85
2 Xeon X5670	51.57	21.04	8.50	3.10	0.95
GTX 480 (monolithic)	36.51	14.66	4.92	1.29	0.29
GTX 295 (monolithic)	33.27	11.40	3.80	1.05	0.24

MP of a GTX480 MP is about on par with a Cell SPE and similar fast to a standard CPU core.

In-depth analysis

Despite different characteristics and implementations, Fermi and CBEA exhibit a very similar compute unit and system performance. The contribution of the various parts of the algorithm to the overall runtime is shown in figure 3.

The initial matrix multiplication is less dominant on the GPU with an extremely high floating point

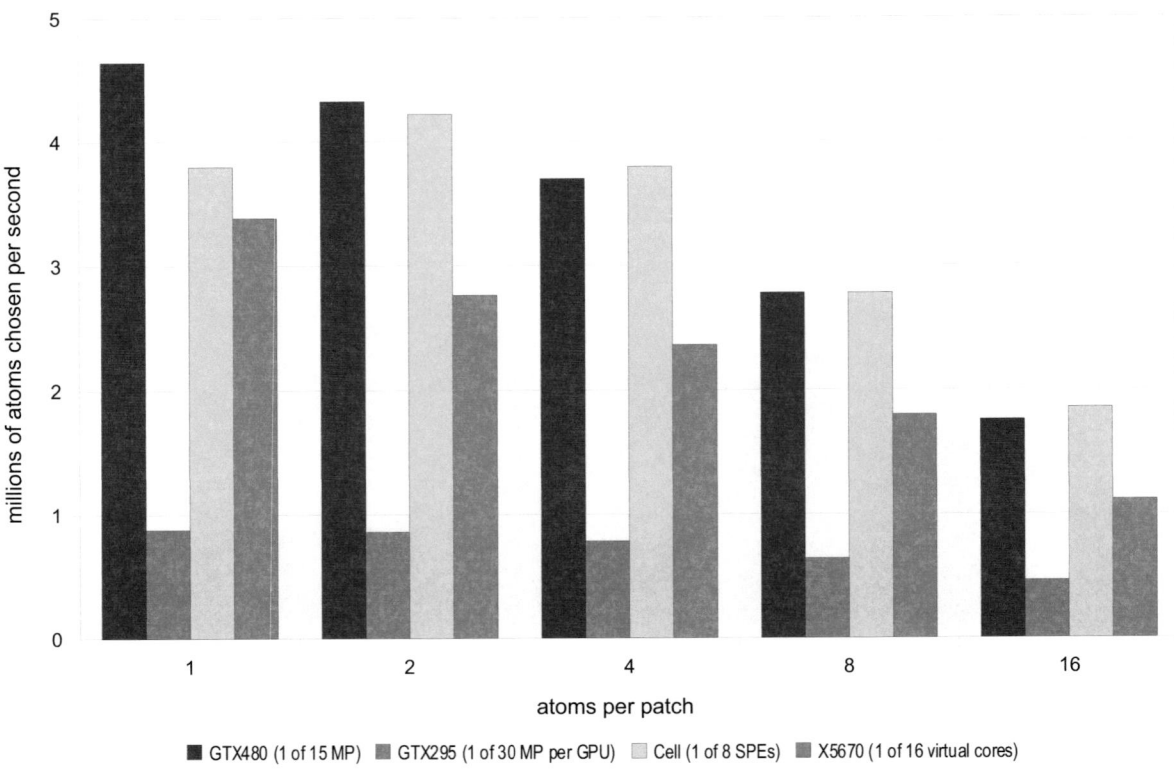

Figure 2. Performance of a single compute unit for the various test platforms, excluding the matrix multiplication.

peak performance, and the rest of initialization (and minor post-processing on the CBEA) hardly affect performance on both architectures.

Finding the next atom is more dominant on the GPU as it is bandwidth limited. NVIDIA's compute profiler estimates a bandwidth of about 132 GB/s for this kernel, but the accumulate bandwidth of 16 SPEs to their local storage is beyond 800 GB/s. The complexity of this task does not grow with the number of atoms already found and its influence therefore vanishes if many atoms should be selected.

Cell has a slight advantage for the projection, once again for its great bandwidth. The profiler estimates the GPU device memory bandwidth to about 50 GB/s, but also detects a L1 cache hit ratio of about 95%. This picture can change if the whole Gram matrix can be cached by a MP or if the dictionary size grows to a size that cannot be held in an SPEs local storage anymore.

The largest difference can be found for the triangular solves: In-order execution and the dedication

to SIMD make it extremely difficult to get good performance on the CBEA, the respective code is manually unrolled and requires a complicated storage scheme for L. Still the performance is far behind the GPU, which is not sensitive to instruction and memory latencies as long as enough parallel computations are in-flight. NVIDIA's profiler measures a device memory bandwidth close to 85 GB/s, with all temporary results being held in shared memory.

Computing the error of the current representation is equally unsuited for both architectures due to the scattered accesses. Their pattern and the memory granularity of at least 32 B for the Fermi architecture lead to low memory bandwidth with low payload. The SPEs with a 16 B granularity to their local storage and better bandwidth lose their advantage by their inability to perform unaligned, scalar loads, which must be imitated by lengthy code.

Depending on their characteristics, the steps of the Batch-OMP algorithm perform quite different

22

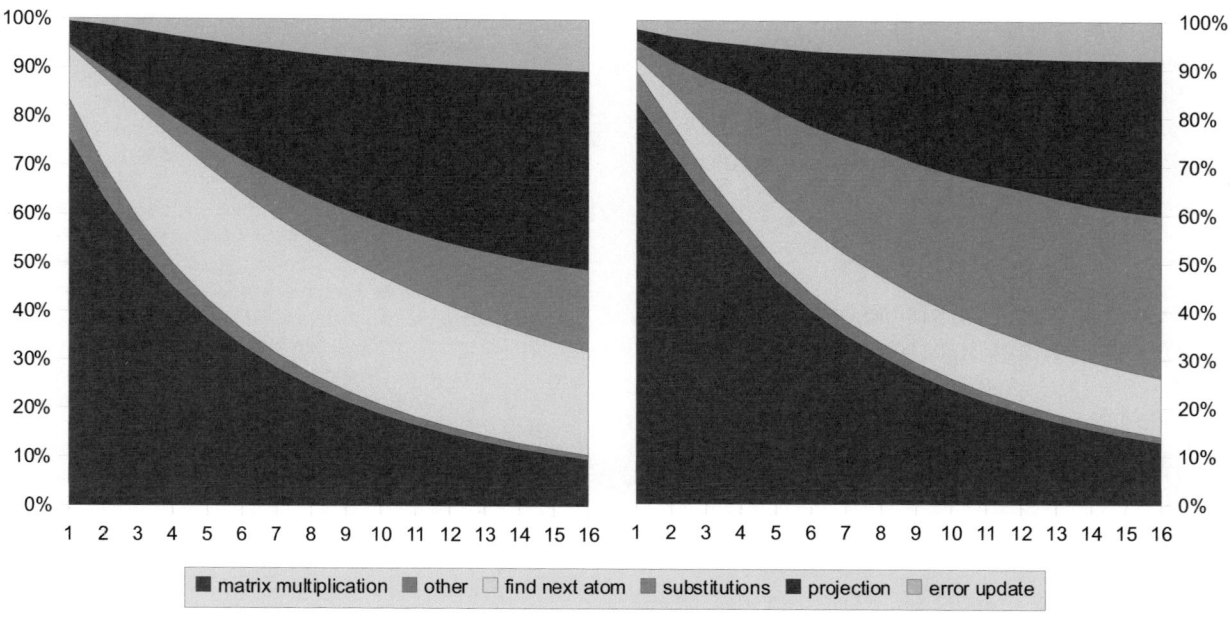

Figure 3. Contribution of the various tasks to the overall runtime depending on number of patches to be chosen for the Fermi architecture (left) and the CBEA (right).

on both platforms. The similar overall runtime performance results from the special mixture of various tasks, where strengths and weaknesses of each architecture balance out.

Resume

Quite obviously, it is not possible to judge the quality of different architectures based on different implementations of a single application. As the Batch-OMP is a more complicated algorithm than typical benchmark kernels, it still gives valuable insights into the features and evolution of the different test platforms.

IBM has announced not to continue CBEA development in its current form, although it is still used in some embedded systems and the Sony PlayStation 3. The current QS22 will most probably be the last representative of Cell in general purpose programming. The performance of this dated platform is still impressive for many applications, also for the Batch-OMP, but comes at a high price not only in terms of money: The separation into slower general purpose and specialized compute cores — the SPEs— with a SIMD-centric ISA and in-order execution causes the worst programmability of all three platforms. Performance is highly dependent on

manual optimization, especially data layout adaptions and SIMD-vectorization. As an example, the C99 kernel getting acceptable performance on the Xeons will perform a magnitude slower on an SPE.

The GTX295 was the top model of NVIDIA's last GPU generation (CUDA compute capability 1.3), while GTX480 was of the first implementation of the newer Fermi GPGPU architecture. It is currently being replaced by the GTX580. One goal of Fermi was to increase generality and programmability, which was reached to some extent. A major factor is the introduction of caches that make caching in shared memory or mapping to texture memory in many cases unnecessary or at least less important. The effort required for programming CUDA mainly depends on how fast a massively parallel formulation of an algorithm is found and how complex it is. However, additional code is always required to manage memory on the GPU and transfer data from and to host memory. Despite its comparably low price, one needs to consider that GPUs only work as accelerators to a host system that needs to run operating system, perform IO, control the execution of kernels, and finally provide power and cooling.

The general purpose workstation required the

least programming effort to get acceptable performance, and could perhaps keep up after further optimization. To accumulate that much compute power in a single system, however, expensive hardware is required – both Xeon processors alone are currently worth about five GTX480.

V. Future Work

We compared the performance of the Batch-OMP algorithm on different hardware architectures. We find that the performance achievable on CBEA, GPGPU and standard CPUs is interestingly similar for this algorithm. We attribute this to the versatile requirements of the various parts of Batch-OMP which cancel out the specifics of each platform.

The next steps are tuning and analysis of the implementation for standard CPUs, and the development of a strategy to compute a different number of atoms on a GPU efficiently.

References

[1] J. Starck, M. Elad, and D. Donoho, "Image decomposition via the combination of sparse representations and a variational approach," *IEEE transactions on image processing*, vol. 14, no. 10, pp. 1570–1582, 2005.

[2] J. Tropp, "Topics in Sparse Approximation," Ph.D. dissertation, The University of Texas at Austin, 2004.

[3] M. Aharon, M. Elad, and A. Bruckstein, "On the uniqueness of overcomplete dictionaries, and a practical way to retrieve them," *Linear Algebra and Its Applications*, vol. 416, no. 1, pp. 48–67, 2006.

[4] G. Davis, S. Mallat, and M. Avellaneda, "Adaptive greedy approximations," *Constructive approximation*, vol. 13, no. 1, pp. 57–98, 1997.

[5] R. Rubinstein, M. Zibulevsky, and M. Elad, "Efficient Implementation of the K-SVD Algorithm and the Batch-OMP Method," Department of Computer Science, Technion, Israel, Tech. Rep., 2008.

[6] A. Borsdorf, R. Raupach, and J. Hornegger, "Wavelet based Noise Reduction by Identification of Correlation," in *Pattern Recognition (DAGM 2006), Lecture Notes in Computer Science*, K. Franke, K. Müller, B. Nickolay, and R. Schäfer, Eds., vol. 4174. Berlin: Springer, 2006, pp. 21–30.

[7] ——, "Separate CT-Reconstruction for 3D Wavelet Based Noise Reduction Using Correlation Analysis," in *IEEE NSS/MIC Conference Record*, B. Yu, Ed., 2007, pp. 2633–2638.

[8] M. Mayer, A. Borsdorf, H. Köstler, J. Hornegger, and U. Rüde, "Nonlinear Diffusion vs. Wavelet Based Noise Reduction in CT Using Correlation Analysis," in *Vision, Modeling, and Visualization 2007*, H. Lensch, B. Rosenhahn, H.-P. Seidel, P. Slusallek, and J. Weickert, Eds., 2007, pp. 223–232.

[9] D. Bartuschat, A. Borsdorf, H. Köstler, R. Rubinstein, and M. Stürmer, "A parallel K-SVD implementation for CT image denoising," Department of Computer Science 10 (System Simulation), Friedrich-Alexander-University of Erlangen-Nuremberg, Germany, Tech. Rep., 2009.

[10] D. Bartuschat, M. Stürmer, and H. Köstler, "An Orthogonal Matching Pursuit Algorithm for Image Denoising on the Cell Broadband Engine," in *Parallel Processing and Applied Mathematics*, ser. Lecture Notes in Computer Science, R. Wyrzykowski, J. Dongarra, K. Karczewski, and J. Wasniewski, Eds. Springer Berlin / Heidelberg, 2010, vol. 6067, pp. 557–566.

[11] A. Borghi, J. Darbon, S. Peyronnet, T. Chan, and S. Osher, "A Compressive Sensing Algorithm for Many-Core Architectures," *Advances in Visual Computing*, pp. 678–686, 2010.

[12] ——, "A simple compressive sensing algorithm for parallel many-core architectures," *CAM Report*, pp. 08–64, 2008.

[13] S. Lee and S. Wright, "Implementing algorithms for signal and image reconstruction on graphical processing units," Computer Sciences Department, University of Wisconsin-Madison, Tech. Rep., 2008.

[14] M. Andrecut, "Fast GPU Implementation of Sparse Signal Recovery from Random Projections," *Arxiv preprint arXiv:0809.1833*, 2008.

[15] A. Septimus and R. Steinberg, "Compressive sampling hardware reconstruction," in *Circuits and Systems (ISCAS), Proceedings of 2010 IEEE International Symposium on*. IEEE, 2010, pp. 3316–3319.

[16] T. R. Braun, "An evaluation of GPU acceleration for sparse reconstruction," in *Signal Processing, Sensor Fusion, and Target Recognition XIX*, I. Kadar, Ed., vol. 7697, no. 15. Proc. of SPIE, 2010, pp. 1–10.

[17] M. Elad and M. Aharon, "Image denoising via sparse and redundant representations over learned dictionaries," *IEEE Trans. Image Process*, vol. 15, no. 12, pp. 3736–3745, 2006.

[18] D. L. Donoho and M. Elad, "Optimally sparse representations in general (non-orthogonal) dictionaries via l^1 minimization," *Proc. Nat. Acad. Sci.*, vol. 100, pp. 2197–2202, 2002.

[19] J. Tropp and A. Gilbert, "Signal recovery from random measurements via orthogonal matching pursuit," *Information Theory, IEEE Transactions on*, vol. 53, no. 12, pp. 4655–4666, 2007.

[20] "Compute Unified Device Architecture, C Programming Guide, version 3.2," *NVIDIA Corporation*, 2010.

Impact of Data Sharing on CMP design: A study based on Analytical Modeling

Anil Krishna, Ahmad Samih, Yan Solihin

Dept. of Electrical and Computer Engineering
North Carolina State University
{akrishn2, aasamih, solihin}@ece.ncsu.edu

Abstract

In this work we study the effect data and instruction sharing on cache miss rates. We then extend an analytical system-level throughput model to take multi-threaded data and instruction sharing into account. We use the model to provide insights into the interaction of thread count, cache size, off-chip bandwidth, and, sharing, on system throughput. Using specific examples we teach how the model can reveal insights about the impact of sharing on questions such as - 1) how should cores in a CMP be sized (fewer larger cores vs. more smaller cores); 2) how many and what configuration CMP chips should be used to build an SMP system given a total thread-count requirement; 3) how do system-level core, cache and bandwidth provisioning decisions change between multi-programmed workloads (as in a cloud computing context) and multi-threaded workloads (as in a commercial or scientific server). Our model reveals that the optimal number and size of cores in a CMP, and the optimal number of CMPs in an SMP, can be significantly different depending of the amount of sharing in the target workload.

Keywords: Chip multiprocessor, Analytical modeling, Data Sharing, Multithreading, Performance

1 Introduction

Over the past few years, Chip Multi Processor(CMP) architecture has become the dominating hardware architecture across a spectrum of computing machinery – personal computing devices, workstations, commercial and scientific servers, and warehouse scale computers. The sheer complexity involved in the design and verification of each unit in a CMP solution has necessitated significant design reuse. The differentiation between computational machinery is orchestrated by careful system-level design choices, while keeping the basic core-level designs relatively unchanged.

Chip and system-level architects make high level design trade-offs during the concept phase and the high level design phase of a project. Some of the design parameters considered by system architects are the number and type of cores used in a CMP, the cache sizes and organization, memory bandwidth, and, on-chip and off-chip interconnect design. Each individual unit on a chip (cores, caches, interconnect, memory controller) is typically designed with extensive simulation driven methodologies. System level design decisions, however, are tackled differently. These are driven more by the target market requirements (performance, energy and cost) and technology limits. Detailed system-level simulations are often not feasible due to simulator complexity, large design spaces, and inordinate simulation turnaround times. This has necessitated the use of less precise, yet more insightful and flexible approaches to system design involving queuing model simulators, spreadsheet analysis, and, analytical modeling.

Analytical modeling of chips and multi-chip systems is a particularly powerful, flexible and insightful approach to design space pruning and performance characterization. There is, however, a need to develop and teach newer ways of using analytical performance models to draw system-level design insights.

Desktop and personal computing applications, which used to be single-threaded, are being rewritten as multi-threaded applications to take advantage of the multiple cores on-chip. CMPs have also enabled a trend in which multi-threaded applications are now moving from the realm of small and medium-size Symmetric Multi Processor (SMP) systems to a single chip. However, though it is tempting to directly transplant, say, a 64-thread medium scale SMP application to a single CMP, the performance impact of such a move is not clear.

CMPs are fundamentally limited by on-chip cache and memory bandwidth compared to an SMP. In fact, as the number of on-chip processing cores grow, they take up corresponding die area from what could have been on-chip cache. Further, more cores without a corresponding increase in the die area place greater pressure on the available on-chip cache resources, leading to greater pressure on the memory bandwidth. This can hurt performance. Therefore, while the achievable performance scalability in SMPs is limited primarily by the inherent scalability limitations in the application itself, with CMPs, another first order concern comes into play – the hardware resources available to each thread with thread scaling.

Multi-threaded applications may be able to withstand this cache and memory bandwidth pressure better compared to multi-programmed workload mixes depending on the amount of instruction and data sharing [1] they exhibit. The prefetching effect of sharing (where one thread fetches data and other threads can use it) can make the on-chip cache behave as an effectively larger cache. This, in turn, may enable additional cores to be added to the chip.

There is a growing need to understand and incorporate the effects of multi-threaded application data sharing into analytical models of chip and multi-chip performance. Developing insights from chip and multi-chip analytical models is an increasingly relevant skill for system-level design.

Most prior work in analytical modeling does not focus on the impact of multi-threaded applications on system-level performance. Prior work has attempted to explore the design considerations in scaling up uni-processor chips into CMPs, primarily assuming multiprogrammed workloads. However, the reverse trend enabled by CMPs, the consolidation of small and medium-scale multi-threaded applications on one or a few CMP chips, has not been explicitly studied.

In this work we first study and classify the impact of data sharing on miss rates for PARSEC 2.1 and NAS parallel benchmarks. We

---

[1] Throughout the rest of the paper the phrase *data sharing* will be used to refer to the sharing of both instructions and data

then extend an existing system-level analytical performance model, with specific focus on multi-threaded applications; we incorporate the impact of data sharing into the analytical model. We illustrate specific examples of how to use the analytical model to draw design insights.

We find that when the system is off-chip bandwidth limited it is possible to increase the core size (and, by extension, core capabilities) to get better single-threaded throughput without any significant loss in overall chip throughput. We discover that Amdahl's Law, which dictates that multi-threaded application performance is constrained by the serial section of code, is significantly less important in on-chip core vs. cache rationing decision when the system is bandwidth constrained. That is, though an application's parallelization efficiency continues to affect the system throughput, in a bandwidth constrained scenario it does not affect the decision of how to divide up die area between cores and cache significantly. We find that when designing a system with a target number of threads, there is an ideal SMP size in a bandwidth constrained scenario. Instead of cramming all the cores on to a single CMP, it may be better, for system throughput, to spread the cores across multiple interconnected CMPs. After a certain amount of SMP scaling, however, there is a distinct knee in the system throughput curve, and any further scaling only results in negligible performance improvement. This may make a case for building SMPs out of CMPs with fewer cores than technologically possible (or, alternatively, using CMPs in which only a subset of the cores are defect-free).

2 Related Work

The popularity of CMPs has encouraged significant research recently in the area of high-level design and resource sizings.

Huh et. al [8] evaluate CMP designs based on two types of processor cores (one in-order and the other about 3x larger, out-of-order core). They predict that the lack of bandwidth scaling hurts CMP scaling, and find that the larger processor core proves to be more area efficient in a bandwidth-constrained scenario. This work is similar to ours in the type of issues addressed. The main difference of our work is that we focus on multi-threaded workloads and try to understand the impact of realistic data sharing in CMP and SMP design, where as this prior work does not model data sharing. A second difference is that we develop and use an analytical model, which may be easier to use than a simulation based study, especially for a large number of on-chip cores.

Alameldeen et al. [1] develop an analytical model, similar in spirit to the model we develop, to study the interplay between cores and caches. They incorporate sharing in their throughput model; however, they only explore a relatively simple sharing pattern (1.3 sharers for any number of threads greater than 1). The focus of their work is to understand the role of cache and link compression in CMP design decisions. Further, though they vary the off-chip bandwidth between 10 GB/s and 10 TB/s, their queuing model is not integrated into their throughput model to mimic a bandwidth-constrained system.

Wentzlaff et al. [17] develop a system-level IPC model, and explore a large space of cache hierarchies for multicores in the cloud computing context. They use SPEC Int 2000 rate applications which have no data sharing. They find that there is a greater leeway in optimizing L1 sizes, but using an optimally-sized L2 is more important. We use their approach to develop our baseline throughput model, and extend it for multi-threaded workloads while incorporating data sharing, parallelizing efficiency and SMP scaling.

Zhao et al. [19] develop a constraint-aware analysis methodology that uses chip area and bandwidth as the two constraints. They explore CMP cache design options, pruning the design space for future Large-scale CMPs (LCMPs). They use an in-house simulation framework, commercial workloads, and restrict the analysis to a fixed number of processor cores per chip (16 or 32). Our work relaxes the core count stipulation and develops an analytical framework to explore additional dimensions in the CMP design space.

Oh et al. [14] explore the cache design space for CMPs with up to 70 processor cores. They explore different cache hierarchies - they consider private, shared (both uniform and non-uniform cache access) and hybrid caches at L2 and L3 levels.

Wu et al. [18] use a simulator to model 1 to 256 processor cores (of a fixed design) in a tiled CMP configuration, running parallel benchmarks. They evaluate the on-chip network contention with cache scaling, and off-chip bandwidth requirements as the number of cores and cache size changes. Their primary goal is to identify whether on-chip communication or off-chip bandwidth will be the main bottleneck to LCMP scaling. They find the off-chip bandwidth to be the bottleneck. They do not explore different core sizes, or the effect of reducing CMP scaling at the expense of increasing SMP scaling.

Rogers et al. [16] use a simple analytical model to highlight the growth in off-chip traffic due to exponential CMP scaling, and then propose techniques (such as 3D stacking, DRAM caches, link compression etc.) to overcome the bandwidth wall for several technology generations. In our work we develop an analytical model to design a CMP or an SMP system in the presence of the bandwidth wall, rather than to prove the severity of the bandwidth wall.

3 Impact of Data Sharing on Miss Rate

Motivation In multi-threaded applications data sharing can help improve cache miss rates. One thread brings the cache block on-chip and one or more threads can then use the cache block without suffering misses. However, as the number of threads grows the competition for the on-chip cache space increases, especially for applications with large working sets. In such a scenario, cache blocks that could have been shared across threads might not stay in the cache long enough to be effective, and the benefit of data sharing declines.

The interaction between the number of threads, the amount of algorithmic sharing potential in an application, and the application's working set size is complex. In order to develop insights into the impact of data sharing on on-chip cache miss rates, in an area-constrained CMP, we use simulation. We then incorporate the findings into an analytical model for chip IPC that we develop in Section 4 and draw insights in Section 6.

Simulated Machine We simulate a CMP under the Virtutech Simics3.1 [12] simulation framework. We assume that each core in the CMP is the same size as 1MB of L2 cache (we elaborate on this assumption in Section 5). We assume that the size of the CMP is the equivalent of 33 Cache Effective Areas (CEAs); a CEA is the size of 1MB of cache. Therefore, the CMP can contain 1 core with 32MB of L2 cache, or, 32 cores and 1 MB of L2 cache, or, any intermediate combination. Each processor core is in-order, single-threaded, and has 32KB each of L1 instruction and data caches. We simulate a shared L2 in order to maximize the potential impact of sharing on the L2 cache miss rates.

We use a total of 20 unique multi-threaded applications from the PARSEC 2.1 [5] and the NAS [4] benchmark suites. We run each application for a billion instructions in the region of interest (i.e.

the parallel region) in order to warm up the on chip caches. We then run the application to the end of the region of interest, or, 10 billion instruction, whichever happens first.

We run each application with 1, 2, 4, 8, 16 and 32 threads (and a correspondingly increasing number of cores and decreasing amount of L2 cache). For each application and thread-count, we measure the L2 miss rates in two ways. In the first case, we simulate an L2 cache where data sharing is allowed as is normal. In a second case, we simulate an L2 cache where data and instruction blocks are treated as being private to the thread that brings the block on-chip. This mimics the effect of running the application without any inter-thread sharing. We then study the relative difference between the miss-rates. We believe that this difference yields an accurate indication of how helpful sharing is in reducing miss rates for different workloads under different thread-scaling scenarios. Prior work has often studied the effect of sharing indirectly, using the sharer count for a cache block. We found that sharer count is an unreliable metric since it does not capture how many misses each shared line saved.

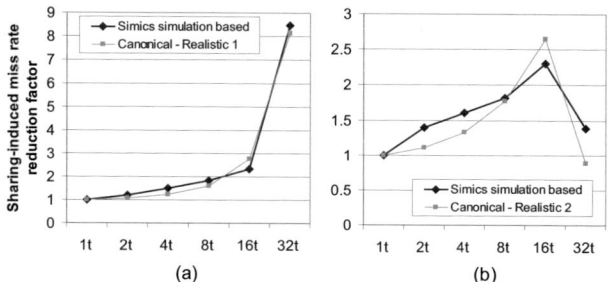

Figure 1. How data sharing affects miss rates.

Result Figure 1 shows how sharing impacts miss-rates. The figure plots relative improvement in miss-rates attributable to sharing (on the y-axis) as the number of threads increases (on the x-axis). The y-axis is normalized to the single-threaded case, which, understandably, involves no sharing, and sees no change in the miss-rate due to sharing. The two sub-plots show the two fundamental behaviors we observed across the 20 benchmarks we studied. Some applications continue to see sharing improve the miss-rates as the number of threads the application is spread across increases. Figure 1(a) plots the average of the following 10 applications which fall under this first category – *blackscholes, bodytrack, facesim, fluidanimate, freqmine, vips, x264, dedup, cg* and *is*. Some applications continue to see sharing improve the miss-rates up to a point, beyond which the beneficial impact of sharing on miss-rates starts to decline. As the number of threads grow inter-thread cache interference makes potential sharing opportunities unrealizable in cache in these workloads. Figure 1(b) plots the average of the following 10 applications which fall under this second category – *ferret, swaptions, canneal, streamcluster, bt, ep, ft, lu, mg* and *sp*. We develop two simple canonical curves to fit the observed sharing-impact - *Realistic1* and *Realistic2*. These are also shown in Figure 1. We use these canonical curves in Section 6, where we study CMP designs using an analytical model; these curves are assumed to represent realistic impact of sharing on miss rates. Further, in order to book-end the impact of sharing we study two additional canonical curves *NoSharing* and *PerfectDoPipe*. Here is a brief description of the canonical curves we use in this work to capture the impact of sharing on cache miss rates.

- *NoSharing*: There is no data sharing between threads. This mimics multi-program workloads, and multi-threaded workloads with minimal sharing.

- *PerfectDoPipe*: The amount of data sharing, and therefore, the effective cache size, grows linearly with the number of threads. That is, only the first thread brings data on-chip and all remaining threads can use that data without suffering any misses. This helps bound multi-threaded performance.

- *Realistic1*: Sharing improves miss-rate (by reducing it) by 7% with every extra thread; this is represented by the canonical curve shown in Figure 1(a).

- *Realistic2*: Sharing improves miss-rate by a fixed amount, equal to 11% of the single-threaded miss-rate for each extra thread for half the maximum number of threads; beyond that, sharing worsens (increases) the miss-rate with an equal-magnitude negative slope. This is represented by the canonical curve as shown in Figure 1(b).

4 Derivation of the Analytical IPC Model

IPC model In this section we develop the analytical model for CMP and SMP system throughput. Our model derivation is based on the approach developed by Wentzlaff et al. [17]. We calculate the Cycles Per Instruction (CPI) for each individual core and then use that to calculate the system-wide throughput. We assume for the purposes of this study that a CMP system is composed of homogeneous cores, and an SMP system is composed of interconnected homogeneous CMPs. Further, we assume that a core is single-threaded; the number of cores corresponds to the number of threads a multi-threaded application can be spread across. Note that if a core under consideration for a design is multi-threaded, then our model can still be used by proportionally dividing the core area by the number of threads per core. Given the per-core CPI (CPI_{core}), and given the number of cores in the system (n), the system-wide IPC (IPC_{system}) is given by Equation 1.

$$IPC_{system} = \frac{n}{CPI_{core}} \qquad (1)$$

Equation 1 is simplistic; it assumes that the performance of a multi-threaded application grows linearly with thread scaling. It has been observed [2] that for multi-threaded workloads realistic scaling is limited by the fraction of the serial section(f_s) in the application code. Taking this into account the system-wide IPC is given by Equation 2.

$$IPC_{system} = \frac{n}{1 + f_s \cdot (n-1)} \cdot \frac{1}{CPI_{core}} \qquad (2)$$

Components of CPI CPI_{core} in Equation 2 is the number of processor cycles it takes to execute an average instruction for a single core. It can be calculated as a summation of the average number of cycles spent by an instruction in three phases - before reaching the L2, in the L2, and, beyond the L2. This is shown in Equation 3.

$$CPI = CPI_{preL2} + CPI_{inL2} + CPI_{beyondL2} \qquad (3)$$

CPI_{preL2} includes the time an instruction spends in the processor core and its reasonably-sized L1s. We assume that CPI_{preL2} can be obtained by system architects, for the core designs under consideration, and the applications under consideration. These can be obtained via detailed simulations or hardware measurements.

27

The CPI_{inL2} term takes into account the cycles an average instruction spends in the L2. Note that the model can be extended to L3 and L4 cache levels in a similar fashion. For the purposes of the high level insights we draw in this paper, we find that a two level cache hierarchy suffices.

The $CPI_{beyondL2}$ depends on application characteristics (the spatial and temporal locality of the application in the L2) as well as microarchitecture characteristics (the per-core L2 size and geometry). We assume that the cache space on the CMP chip is divided evenly across the cores as private L2 caches. We assume that for a given application and a given core design, the number of L2 accesses per instruction(api_{L2}) is a metric that is available to a system architect from simulation or measurement. Every access to the L2 spends the time to look-up the L2, regardless of whether it is a hit or a miss. This latency is dependent on the L2 cache size. We leave the latency term as function of the cache size. When using the formula we plug in latency values calculated by CACTI6.5 [7] for the appropriate cache size.

For both the CPI_{inL2} and $CPI_{beyondL2}$ (which refers to the cycles spent by an average instruction in the memory subsystem lower than the L2), we first need the per-core L2 cache size.

Per-core L2 Size We assume that the CMP is composed of CEA_T units of area, where each unit of area is the equivalent of 1MB of cache. We use 1MB only because it is a reasonably small area in process technologies of today, and gives us a fine grain unit of area to work with. We refer to these grains of chip area as Cache Equivalent Areas(CEAs). We assume that system architects start with some rough estimate of the total chip area, based on process yield estimates, chip power budget etc. We assume that the CEA_T CEAs of area corresponds to the total chip area to be devoted to cores and L2 cache (L1 cache is included in core area). We assume that each core is CEA_p CEAs in size (fractional values allowed). Given n cores in a chip, the amount of cache per core ($L2_{core}$) can be calculated as shown by Equation 4.

$$L2_{core} = \frac{CEA_T - CEA_p \cdot n}{n} \quad (4)$$

The $L2_{core}$ is a unitless quantity, and represents the number of CEAs (each CEA is equal to the size of a 1MB cache array) that make up the per-core L2 cache size.

Returning to the second term in Equation 3, we can now represent CPI_{inL2} as shown in Equation 5, where, $t_{hit}()$ represents the function that takes in the cache size and returns the hit latency.

$$CPI_{inL2} = api_{L2} \cdot t_{hit}(L2_{core} \cdot 1MB) \quad (5)$$

The third term in Equation 3 is $CPI_{beyondL2}$, and is perhaps the most interesting as memory system bandwidth is likely to become a constrained resource in the future. The number of cycles an average instruction spends beyond the L2 depends, firstly, on how often it misses the L2, and, secondly, on how long does it take to return after a miss. *How often* the average instruction misses the L2 depends on how often the average instruction accesses the L2 (a parameter we have seen before, api_{L2}) and the application's L2 miss-rate. *How long* the average instruction takes beyond a miss is the sum of the time an instruction spends queued up trying to get to memory(T_Q), and the memory access penalty(T_M). We put these together into Equation 6, where $f_{miss}()$ represents a function which takes the per-core L2 size and appropriate workload characteristics into consideration and generates the cache miss-rate.

$$CPI_{beyondL2} = api_{L2} \cdot f_{miss}(workload, L2_{core} \cdot 1MB) \cdot (T_M + T_Q) \quad (6)$$

L2 Miss Rate and Data Sharing We use the well-known Power Law of cache miss-rates [6], and, the canonical sharing-impact curves from Section 3, to replace $f_{miss}()$ in Equation 6 with. We assume that α, the workload's sensitivity to cache size changes, and m_{1MB}, the miss-rate of the application with a 1MB L2 cache, are both easily obtainable quantities from measurement or simulation. Further, we assume that $E(n)$ represents the canonical sharing-impact curves for a given workload as a function of n, the number of threads the workload is spread across. Equation 7 shows the updated equation.

$$CPI_{beyondL2} = api_{L2} \cdot m_{1MB} \cdot L2_{core}^{-\alpha} \cdot E(n) \cdot (T_M + T_Q) \quad (7)$$

Misses Per Instruction It is useful to recognize that without the $(T_M + T_Q)$ term the right side of Equation 7 represents the L2 misses per instruction. Equation 8 extracts this metric (MPI_{L2}) explicitly.

$$MPI_{L2} = api_{L2} \cdot m_{1MB} \cdot L2_{core}^{-\alpha} \cdot E(n) \quad (8)$$

Memory Latency The memory penalty, T_M, in Equation 7 is, typically, a well understood constant. Coherence protocol overheads and average on-chip network delays (often, tens of processor clocks) may be added to the pure memory penalty (often, hundreds of processor clocks) to get T_M.

Memory Queuing Delay To calculate T_Q, we assume a standard M/D/1 queuing model to represent the memory interconnect. The mean service rate, μ, is a constant depending on the rate at which the interconnect can transfer a request. We assume that the off-chip bandwidth in one direction in B GB/s and that the processor frequency is f GHz. Thus the service rate in bytes per cycle is B/f overall, and $1/n$ of that per core.

We model the arrival of memory requests as a Poisson process, with a mean arrival rate of λ. The mean arrival rate in bytes per cycle depends on the request rate (in request per cycle) and the request size (in bytes per request). The request size is simply the L2 block size (l_{L2} bytes). The request rate in requests per cycle, can be calculated from the L2 misses per instruction (MPI_{L2}) and the cycles per instruction (CPI_{core}). Equation 9 summarizes this.

$$\mu = \frac{B}{f \cdot n}, \lambda = \frac{MPI_{L2}}{CPI_{core}} \quad (9)$$

For an M/D/1 queue, the queuing delay(T_Q), is given by Equation 10, where ρ refers to $\frac{\lambda}{\mu}$.

$$T_Q = \frac{\rho}{2\mu(1 - \rho)} \quad (10)$$

Substituting from Equation 9 into Equation 10, and simplifying it, we get to Equation 11.

$$T_Q = \frac{MPI_{L2} \cdot f^2 \cdot n^2}{2 \cdot B^2 \cdot CPI_{core} - 2 \cdot B \cdot f \cdot n \cdot MPI_{L2}} \quad (11)$$

Final CPI Model Now we have all the components of Equation 3. Equation 12 puts it all together.

$$CPI_{core} = CPI_{preL2} + (api_{L2} \cdot t_{hit}(L2_{core} \cdot 1MB)) +$$
$$MPI_{L2} \cdot (T_M + \frac{MPI_{L2} \cdot f^2 \cdot n^2}{2 \cdot B^2 \cdot CPI_{core} - 2 \cdot B \cdot f \cdot n \cdot MPI_{L2}}) \quad (12)$$

We leave the $L2_{core}$ and MPI_{L2} terms unexpanded. We can see that the CPI_{core} term appears on both sides of equation. In particular, the T_Q term is inversely proportional to CPI_{core}. This is expected and insightful. It indicates that as the off-chip queuing delay (T_Q) increases, the instruction processing rate slows down and CPI_{core} increases. However, an increasing CPI_{core} slows down the rate at which requests are made to the memory subsystem; this helps the queued up requests drain and improves T_Q.

We ignore the on-chip network queuing, which, being not pinbound, tends to scale much better than off-chip bandwidth.

It is also clear from studying Equation 12 that when workload-specific parameters (α, m_{1MB}, api_{L2}, $E(n)$), the microarchitecture-and-workload-specific parameter (CPI_{preL2}), the technology process specific parameter ($t_{hit}()$) and design specific variables (CEA_T, n, CEA_p) are all set, we end up with a quadratic equation in CPI_{core}. This can be solved by using the standard quadratic equation solution, taking care that the + form of the solution is used [17].

5 Assumptions

The model developed in Section 4 has many parameters. Depending on the process technology, area budget, workload characteristics, core microarchitecture, and power or energy constraints, several parameters in the model can be fixed, allowing the model to explore a relevant and focused solution space. In this section we describe the specific parameter assumptions that we make for the analysis in Section 6.

We assume a 22nm process technology. We assume that the chip size devoted to cores and lower level cache is around $307mm^2$. The actual chip die area is larger, by about 25%, to account for on-chip interconnect, memory controllers and other pervasive logic. Using CACTI6.5 [7] we calculate [2] that 1MB of SRAM cache occupies about $1.2mm^2$ (we assume 8-way set associativity), giving us about 256 CEAs (a CEA is equal to 1MB of cache).

For the baseline core microarchitecture, we use area estimates from IBM's latest embedded processor core, PPC476FP [10] (out-of-order, multi-issue superscalar, single-threaded core, with Floating Point support), ARM's Cortex A9 core [3] (out-of-order, multi-issue superscalar, with Floating Point support) and MIPS 1004K core [13] (in-order, dual-core design with dual-threading per core, with floating point support). We find that at 1.2 to $1.5mm^2$ (in 22nm technology) there are several baseline core designs which can be used as a building block for CMP or an SMP. This baseline core choice allows us to approximate CEA_p, the number of CEAs needed per core, to 1. We will relax this restriction and approximate the impact of going to larger and smaller cores in Section 6.3.

For the workload characteristics we assume a memory intensive workload. We assume an api_{L2}, the probability of an average instruction accessing the L2, of 0.033. This corresponds to the api_{L2} we measured for *canneal, facesim, swaptions* and *x264* benchmarks. Most other workloads we studied have a much smaller rate to access to the L2. However, we intentionally choose a memory intensive workload to illustrate the impact of sharing, while the memory system is stressed. We assume a m_{1MB}, the miss-rate with a 1MB L2 cache, of 0.6. This corresponds to highly memory intensive, data streaming workloads where there is a large working set and little reuse. We made the decision to go with such an example to more clearly illustrate high-level insights in Section 6, effects may be more subtle if less memory intensive parameters are chosen. We assume the standard $\sqrt{2}$ miss-rate sensitivity [6] for the power law (α=0.5). We set CPI_{preL2} to 2 (varied in Section 6.3).

---

[2]CACTI6.5 provides latency and area estimates only down to 32nm process technology; we measure area and latency for different cache sizes for 90nm, 65nm, 45nm and 32nm technologies and extrapolate these to 22nm.

According to the projections from ITRS [11] chip pin-counts are growing at a rate of 5% per year. For a cost-effective bus signaling solution, the rate of growth of bus frequency is about 10%. This falls significantly short of the 59% per year growth in transistor density which is expected to continue for at least another decade. In order to highlight this bandwidth wall, we assume that the off-chip bandwidth is 30 GBps (15 GBps in each direction). This is similar to the usable bandwidth available with a 128-bit dual-channel DDR3-1066. We assume that the processor frequency is 2GHz, the memory penalty (including coherence protocol overheads, on-chip network delay, memory controller and memory device overhead) is 400 processor clocks, and the L2 cache line size is 128 bytes.

We assume, as a baseline, that the multi-threaded code can be perfectly parallelized (f_s, serial fraction = 0); however, we relax this in Section 6.2 to study the impact of parallelization efficiency. We study data sharing as suggested by the 4 canonical sharing-impact curves identified in Section 3 – NoSharing, PerfectDoPipe, Realistic1 and Realistic2. We extend these curves to applications that scale to 256 threads (compared to the 32 threads that the curves were originally generated with). We realize that the specific benchmarks we studied in Section 3 may not be scalable to 256 threads; however, similar sharing patterns may still provide valuable insights into how sharing impacts design choices.

6 Evaluation and Analysis

In this section we use the analytical throughput model from Section 4 and the design space parameter assumptions from Section 5 to develop both design insights and provide examples of how the model may be used.

6.1 Effect of off-chip bandwidth

Using Equation 12 with and without the T_Q term (off-chip queuing delay), we get the per-core CPI (CPI_{core}) in the bandwidth limited (30 GBps) and the infinite bandwidth scenarios respectively. Using Equation 2, and assuming perfect parallelism (a constraint we relax in section 6.2), we can estimate the best-case chip-wide IPC. We vary the number of cores, n, from 1 (almost all-cache) to a maximum of 255 (almost all-cores). Figure 2 contains 4 plots, one for each of the 4 sharing patterns we study. The plots show the number of processor cores (out of a maximum of 256) on the x-axis and the chip IPC on the y-axis.

There are two main observations that can be drawn from these plots. First, in a bandwidth-constrained system the optimal core count can be *significantly* smaller than in a non-bandwidth-constrained system (47 vs 220 with a Realistic1 sharing assumption). This observation, by itself, is not novel; however, the model's agreement with prior observations [8, 18, 16] is comforting. Second, even with reasonably good amount of sharing (Realistic1 and Realistic2) the optimal core count does not increase as much in a bandwidth-constrained system, compared to the NoSharing case. With Realistic1 and Realistic2 sharing-impact, only an extra 9 and 7 cores may be added respectively, to the optimal core-count in the NoSharing case. Similarly, the best achievable IPC can be vastly different across different sharing behaviors; however, in a constrained bandwidth scenario IPC is much less sensitive to sharing behavior.

In summary, these figures indicate that though data sharing has the potential to allow the integration of a lot more cores on chip compared to a workload mix with no sharing (and thus benefit from the resultant IPC improvement), in a bandwidth constrained system only a small fraction of this potential gain may be realized.

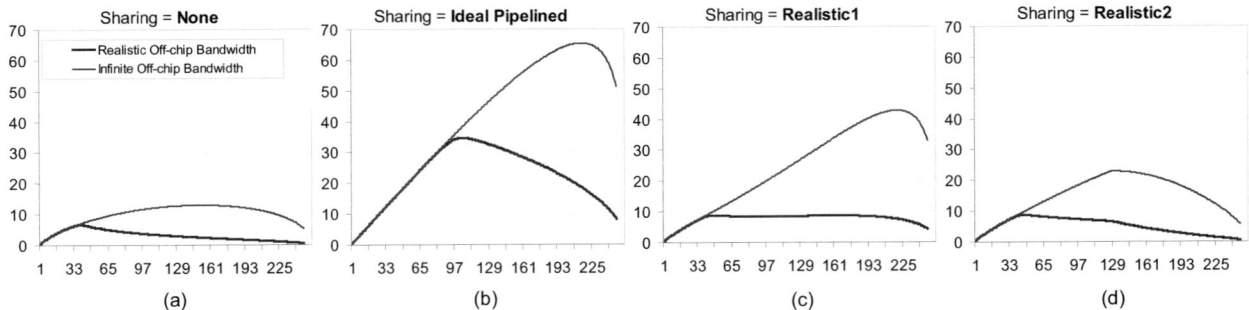

Figure 2. Effect of off-chip bandwidth on CMP scaling. The x-axis is the number of cores and the y-axis is chip IPC

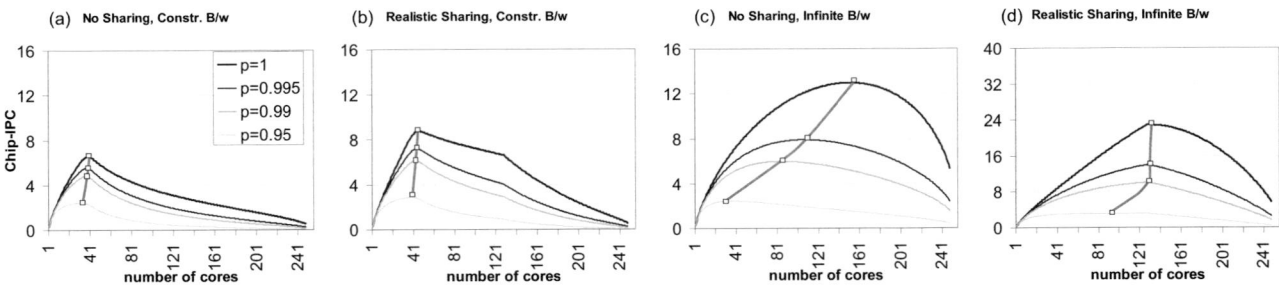

Figure 3. Core-count that maximizes chip-IPC is less sensitive to parallelization efficiency in a bandwidth-constrained system.

6.2 Effect of Amdahl's Law

Amdahl's Law [2], when applied to performance scaling of a multi-threaded program, states that the serial section of code significantly affects the realizable speed-up as parallel programs scale to a larger number of threads. We study the impact of this by varying the fraction of serial section in workloads between 0%, 0.5%, 1% and 5% in Equation 2. Figure 3 shows the chip IPC curves for the 4 parallelization efficiencies. There are 4 plots. The first pair of plots assumes a bandwidth-constrained scenario; the second pair assumes an infinite bandwidth scenario. In each pair, the first plot depicts the NoSharing scenario and the second plot depicts the Realistic1 sharing pattern. The x-axis is the number of cores on-chip (out of a maximum of 256). The y-axis plots the chip IPC.

The figure shows that data sharing improves chip IPC significantly, and parallelization efficiency affects chip IPC noticeably. However, the main takeaway from this figure is that the peaks of the IPC curves fall along an almost vertical line on the left two curves. This indicates that the optimal core-count decision does not change much with parallelization efficiency in a bandwidth-constrained scenario. We deal with a bandwidth-constrained system in the later sections; therefore, we assume 100% parallelization efficiency, without affecting the correctness of the decisions related to core vs cache rationing.

A second important observation from this figure is seen from the rightmost two plots. When there is sufficient bandwidth, the benefit of sharing is better realized in workloads which are more efficiently parallelized. With 95% parallel code the IPC only improves 1.30X going from NoSharing to Realistic1. However, with 99%, 99.5% and 100% parallel code the improvement is 1.68X, 1.77X and 1.76X respectively.

In summary, in a bandwidth-constrained system the core vs. cache decision is roughly parallelization-efficiency independent. In a non-bandwidth-constrained system the impact of data sharing on chip throughput is directly correlated with the parallelization efficiency.

6.3 Effect of Core Size

System architects often face a situation where they need to pick a core design from several baseline core designs to integrate into a CMP. Our baseline core size is equal to 1 CEA (CEA_p=1). We relax this restriction in this section to study the effect of integrating smaller or larger cores in a CMP. We try CEA_p values of 0.25, 0.5, 1 (baseline), 2, 4 and 8. We assume, in accordance with Pollack's Rule [15], that a core K times larger than a base design (therefore, K times more complex) provides only a $\sqrt{K}$ improvement in performance. Doubling the core size boosts IPC by approximately 41%, while halving the size of a core reduces IPC to about 71%, of initial value. Figure 4 plots the best chip-wide IPC and the corresponding per-core IPC for 6 different core designs, each under the Realistic2 and NoSharing scenarios. The core sizes (in CEAs) and their corresponding expected CPI_{preL2}s are shown on the x-axis. With NoSharing, the chip IPC reduces somewhat with smaller cores; however, the drop is more steep with 4x and 8x larger cores. There is an 8% drop in chip IPC by going to cores 0.25x the base line size. With the Realistic2 sharing, there is no loss in chip wide IPC by moving to smaller cores. However, for this to be realized, applications must be parallelizable across hundreds of threads, which may not be practical. When the core size is increased to 2x the base size, the per-core IPC improves considerably (14%), for a relatively small loss in chip IPC. Note that with larger cores, the *number* of cores reduces compared to the core-count with smaller cores. Therefore, for applications which may be single threaded

30

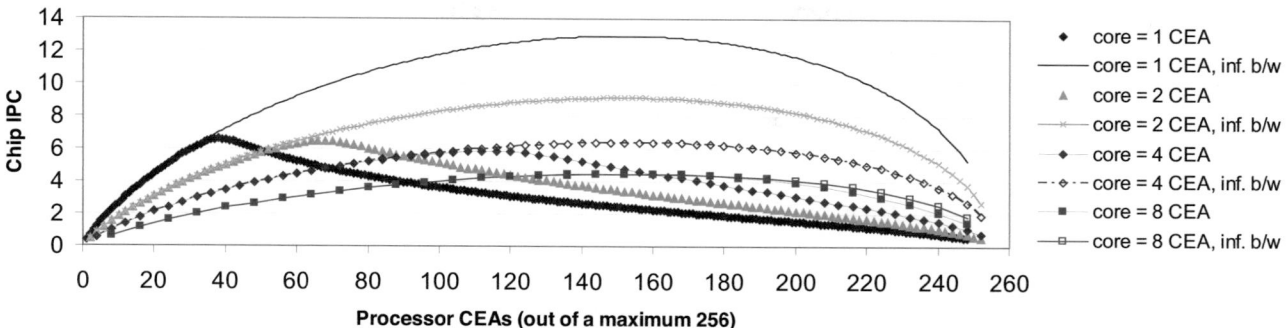

Figure 5. Effect of increasing core size on the bandwidth and cache walls

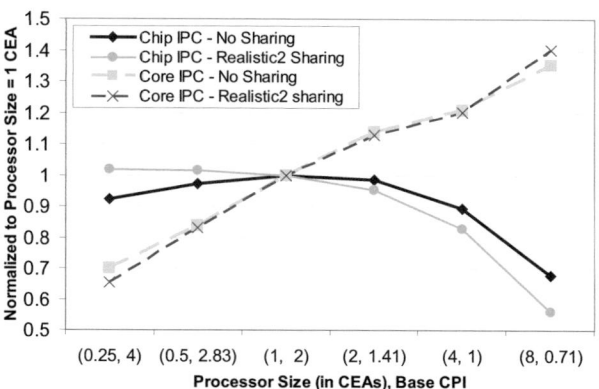

Figure 4. Effect of core type on overall, and per-core, throughput

or scale to a smaller degree of parallelism, larger cores may make sense.

Figure 5 shows the underlying reason for why fewer larger cores may do just as well as more smaller cores. The figure plots the CEAs devoted to processor logic along the x-axis (note that 1 CEA no longer necessarily corresponds to 1 core). The y-axis is the chip IPC. The per-core IPC is not explicitly plotted; it is understood that a larger core will have a better core IPC. There are 8 series in the plot. The IPC curves are plotted for core sizes of 1, 2, 4 and 8 CEAs, each with and without the bandwidth constraint. As can be seen from the figure, there are two main effects of going to larger cores. First, the fraction of chip area occupied by cores increases. This is because there are fewer cores, and they need lesser cache compared to the case with smaller cores occupying the same amount of total core area. This frees up more area for the cores to occupy. Second, the chip IPC falls. This too happens because there are fewer cores, and the individual core's IPC does not grow in proportion to the core's size. However, because of the bandwidth-constrained nature of the design space, the reduction in the best-case chip IPC, especially going from 1 to 2 CEAs per core, is negligible. As the cores get larger, the difference between the peaks of the bandwidth-constrained and the non-bandwidth-constrained curves get closer. In other words, as the number of processors reduces the bandwidth wall becomes less severe (compared to the cache wall). This makes a case for moving to larger processors rather than scaling to a larger number of processors in the presence of the bandwidth wall.

In summary, there may be an optimal core size which gives the best single-threaded performance without hurting chip IPC noticeably.

6.4 SMP Scaling

So far we have used our model to draw insights about CMP design. Another interesting area that the model can help explore is SMP to CMP consolidation. With CMPs becoming the industry standard for all computing platforms, and CMP-scaling continuing in the foreseeable future, server-consolidation is generating widespread interest. CMPs are being seen as a vehicle to assimilate SMPs by effectively creating an SMP on-chip. With IBM's 8-core POWER7 system already announced [9], and with more scaling likely in the future, a small to medium scale SMP could fit on a single chip. To study the impact of such an SMP to CMP consolidation, we take as an example a system which expects to use 200 threads. The system designer has the option of either placing all the 200 threads on one CMP (across 200 $CEA_p=1$ cores), or spreading the cores across multiple tightly interconnected CMPs. We continue to assume a bandwidth-constrained system. We further assume that with each additional CMP that is added to the SMP system the additional pin resources provide another 30 GBps of bandwidth to the distributed memory. We ignore the additional network delay to get to the appropriate SMP node. [3]

Figure 6 shows the system IPC (across the SMP) when 200 cores are spread across 1 through 8 CMP chips. There are 4 series plotted, corresponding to the 4 sharing scenarios we study. Focusing first on the NoSharing curve, the figure shows that instead of placing all the 200 cores on one CMP (which is possible, but performance suffers significantly due to the bandwidth limitation), it is better to spread the 200 cores across multiple chips.

In fact, performance improves almost linearly up to about a 6-way SMP, beyond which performance starts to saturate. There are 2 reasons for why spreading the cores across multiple CMPs improves performance. First, by reducing the number of cores on each chip, both the total cache on-chip and the per core cache increases. This reduces the pressure on off-chip bandwidth significantly. Second, every new CMP brings with it additional pins and, therefore, additional bandwidth. After about 5 to 6 chips, however, spreading cores on to additional chips does not give proportional performance benefit because the SMP as a whole has overcome the bandwidth wall. The additional chips do add more cache, leading to monotonically increasing performance. We model a small scale SMP system. For larger SMP systems, a more robust representation of the effect of the interconnect becomes important, and hence it would not be sur-

---

[3]We experimented by increasing the T_M term in Equation 6 by 50 and 100 pClks to account for both the increase in average memory latency and the coherence overhead, and found that both qualitatively and quantitatively the results are not affected significantly.

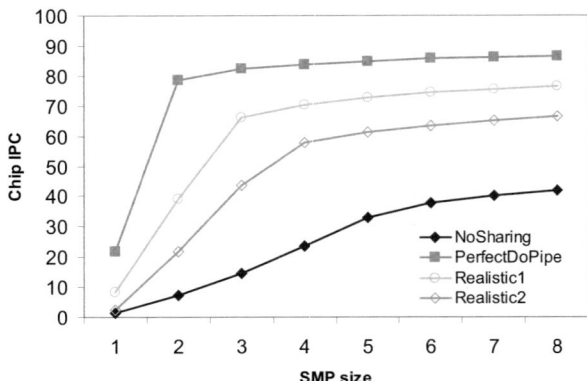

Figure 6. Scaling the number of chips in an SMP system

prising if the system IPC starts to degrade as scaling spreads across more chips.

With Realistic1 and Realistic2 sharing scenarios, the effect of going from 1 CMP with 200 cores to 2 chips with 100 cores on each, is even more dramatic. In fact, at a 3-way SMP with about 67 cores per chip for Realistic1 (4-way with 50 cores per chip for Realistic2), there is a distinct performance knee. This figure shows that sharing can significantly help reduce the size of an SMP system. Effectively, these curves tell us that in a bandwidth-constrained scenario, where the total number of cores is known *a priori* the cost trade-off is between spreading the work across multiple chips versus providing a more expensive, higher bandwidth memory bus and multiple memory controllers to provide the necessary off-chip bandwidth. There are at least three issues to consider. First, with fewer cores needed per chip, the CMP yields may be much better, thus making each chip cheaper. Second, with fewer cores per chip, the chip will likely run cooler, thus saving packaging and cooling costs. Third, with the extra pins available with the extra chips, the memory bus can be operated at a lower frequency (and lower power) using standard single-ended signaling technology (rather than, say, a higher-frequency, differential signaling, technology).

In fact, Figure 6 may also make the case to reduce the area of the CMP chip. There are fewer cores in each CMP in the optimal design. The performance of the SMP is more sensitive to off-chip bandwidth increase than cache increase that comes with more chips (the cache sensitivity is visible in the slowly growing tails of the curves in this figure). Therefore, it may be possible to reduce the chip size noticeably by reducing the on-chip cache, while retaining the core count. We leave this study for future work.

In summary, to enable a targeted number of cores/threads in a system there exists a certain minimum number of chips across which the cores/threads should be spread for best overall throughput; scaling beyond that results in almost no further performance gain.

7 Conclusion

CMP design in the future will rely on core-level design-reuse to provide chip-level design-differentiation. Multi-threaded workloads require a new dimension, data-sharing, to be considered in chip design. In this work we studied how data sharing impacts cache miss rates of multithreaded workloads. Then wei extended a simple, but powerful, analytical, throughput model that can help system architects explore the interplay of design parameters, such as - number

and size of cores, workload characteristics, and, cache and memory organizations. We incorporated the effect of multi-threaded data sharing into the analytical model. The model revealed interesting insights. For example, the model revealed that though data sharing can significantly boost throughput compared to an application whose threads do not share data, in a bandwidth-constrained scenario, the benefit from sharing is severely restricted. The model also showed that in future, off-chip bandwidth constrained systems, it may be possible to use fewer larger cores to build a CMP, rather than many smaller cores, without reducing the chip throughput.

References

[1] A. R. Alameldeen. *Using Compression to Improve Chip Multiprocessor Performance*. PhD thesis, University of Wisconsin at Madison, 2006.

[2] G. M. Amdahl. Validity of the single processor approach to achieving large scale computing capabilities. In *AFIPS Conf. Proc.*, pages 483–485, 1967.

[3] ARM. Corex A9 Processor. http://www.arm.com/products/processors/cortex-a/cortex-a9.php, 2010.

[4] D. Bailey, et al. The NAS Parallel Benchmarks. *Intl. Journal of Supercomputer Applications*, 5(3):63–73, 1991.

[5] C. Bienia, S. Kumar, J. P. Singh, and K. Li. The PARSEC Benchmark Suite: Characterization and Architectural Implications. In *17th Intl. Conf. on Parallel Architectures and Compilation Techniques*, 2008.

[6] A. Hartstein, V. Srinivasan, T. Puzak, and P. Emma. On the Nature of Cache Miss Behavior: Is It $\sqrt{2}$? In *The Journal of Instruction-Level Parallelism*, volume 10, pages 1–22, 2008.

[7] Hewlett Packard Laboratories. CACTI6.5. http://www.hpl.hp.com/research/cacti/, 2010.

[8] J. Huh, D. Burger, and S. W. Keckler. Exploring the Design Space of Future CMPs. In *2001 Intl. Conf. on Parallel Architectures and Compilation Techniques*, pages 199–210, 2001.

[9] IBM. POWER7. http://www-03.ibm.com/press/us/en/pressrelease/29315.wss, 2009.

[10] IBM. PowerPC 476FP. http://www.power.org/events/powercon09/taiwan09/IBM_Overview_PowerPC476FP.pdf, 2009.

[11] ITRS. International Technology Roadmap for Semiconductors: 2007 Edition, Assembly and Packaging. http://www.itrs.net/Links/2007ITRS/2007Chapters/2007Assembly.pdf, 2007.

[12] P. S. Magnusson, M. Christensson, J. Eskilson, D. Forsgren, G. Hallberg, J. Hogberg, F. Larsson, A. Moestedt, and B. Werner. Simics: A Full System Simulation Platform. *Computer*, 35:50–58, 2002.

[13] MIPS. MIPS 1004K Processor. http://www.mips.com/products/processors/32-64-bit-cores/mips32-1004k, 2010.

[14] T. Oh, H. Lee, K. Lee, and S. Cho. An Analytical Model to Study Optimal Area Breakdown between Cores and Caches in a Chip Multiprocessor. In *2009 IEEE Computer Society Symp. on VLSI*, pages 181–186, 2009.

[15] F. J. Pollack. New microarchitecture challenges in the coming generations of CMOS process technologies (keynote address). In *32nd annual ACM/IEEE international symposium on Microarchitecture*, pages 2–, 1999.

[16] B. M. Rogers, A. Krishna, G. B. Bell, K. Vu, X. Jiang, and Y. Solihin. Scaling the Bandwidth Wall: Challenges in and Avenues for CMP Scaling. In *36th Intl. Symp. on Computer Architecture*, pages 371–382, 2009.

[17] D. Wentzlaff, N. Beckmann, J. Miller, and A. Agarwal. Core Count vs Cache Size for Manycore Architectures in the Cloud. Tech. Rep. MIT-CSAIL-TR-2010-008, MIT, 2010.

[18] M.-J. Wu and D. Yeung. Scaling Single-Program Performance on Large-Scale Chip Multiprocessors. Tech. Rep. UMIACS-TR-2009-16, University of Maryland, 2009.

[19] L. Zhao and R. Iyer, et al. Performance, Area, and Bandwidth Implications for Large scale CMP Cache Design. In *CMP-MSI*, 2007.

Traffic Prediction for NoCs using Fuzzy Logic

Gervin Thomas   Ben Juurlink
Technische Universität Berlin
Department of Computer Engineering and Microelectronics
Embedded Systems Architectures
Berlin, Germany
Email: {gthomas,juurlink}@cs.tu-berlin.de

Dietmar Tutsch
Bergische Universität Wuppertal
Automation / Computer Science
Wuppertal, Germany
Email: tutsch@uni-wuppertal.de

Abstract—Networks on Chip provide faster communication and higher throughput for chip multiprocessor systems than conventional bus systems. Having multiple processing elements on one chip, however, leads to a large number of message transfers in the NoC. The consequence is that more blocking occurs and time and power is wasted with waiting until the congestion is dissolved. With knowledge of future communication patterns, blocking could be avoided. Therefore, in this paper a model is introduced to predict future communication patterns to avoid network congestion. Our model uses a fuzzy based algorithm to predict end-to-end communication. The presented model accurately predictions for up to 10 time intervals for continuous patterns. Communication patterns with non-continuous behaviors, such as fast changes from peak to zero, can also be predicted accurately for the next 1 to 2 time intervals to come. The model is a first step to predict future communication patterns. In addition, some limitations are identified that must be solved in order to improve the model.

I. INTRODUCTION

Increasing the clock frequency to increase performance is no longer an option due to, amongst others, energy consumption, heat developments, and the enormous costs for new technologies [1] [2]. To increase the performance of a chip, processor vendors integrate more cores on one die. The current trend is that the number of cores on a chip multiprocessor (CMP) increases with every new generation and so parallel computing has become more important than ever. The increasing number of cores requires a communication system different from a conventional bus system, since a bus quickly becomes the bottleneck of the system. One approach is to employ a Network on Chip (NoC). With the ongoing trend to increase the number of cores on CMPs, the NoC becomes an essential part of the system.

There are many NoC topologies such as meshes, trees, multi-stage interconnection networks (MINs), and many more. NoCs have several advantages such as scalability and modularity. The optimal network configuration depends on the application that is running because every application produces different traffic patterns and, moreover, these patterns may change over time. The NoC should realize communications with minor congestion or, if possible, free of congestion. Otherwise, the communication between cores may become the bottleneck. Several researcher [3] [4] have proposed reconfigurable networks to establish communication paths without congestion. The challenge of establishing congestion-free communication depends on the applications that run on the system. Often, congestion arises because several cores send messages at the same time and all messages must be routed through the same network. If two or more messages arrive at the same time at the same switching element and compete for the same link, only one can pass while the others must wait. This situation could be avoided if, before the communication starts, it is already known how much data each core will send and to which core. In that case the routing in the network could be realized with minor congestion by changing the routing algorithm. As another example, if the NoC has a reconfigurable structure, disjoint or lightly loaded paths through the network could be established.

This work presents a method to predict end-to-end communication patterns. Our method is based on a fuzzy algorithm. The prediction method searches for similar pattern in the communication history and predicts based on that information the next data point. By taking the newly predicted data point into account and applying this technique several times, several future steps can be predicted. The method is validated with a chaotic time series and with some real traffic traces obtained on a multicore system.

This paper is organized as follows. Section II describes related work. Section III provides a motivational example and Section IV describes the model that is applied. Section V describes the fuzzy based algorithm that is used to predict end-to-end traffic. Results are presented in Section VI. Finally, Section VII summarizes the paper and presents some directions for future work.

II. RELATED WORK

Huang et al. [5] proposed a table-driven predictor to predict communication in NoCs. Like us, they predicted end-to-end traffic without taking intermediate switches into account. Their method, however, only predicted one future time interval. The predicted amount of communication is either zero or the current quantity. The technique was evaluated by running a modified block LU decomposition kernel on Tilera's TILE64 platform. Kaxiras and Young [6] used coherence communication prediction in distributed shared-memory systems to detect data that is needed by several processors and to deliver the data as soon as possible. Their approach is also table-driven. Duato and Lysne [7] [8] have proposed a methodology for deriving procedures for dynamic and deadlock-free reconfiguration between routing functions but did not used any prediction technique.

Ahmad [3] introduced a dynamically reconfigurable NoC architecture for reconfigurable Multiprocessor system-on-chip. Hansson and Goossens [4] introduced a library for NoC reconfiguration for dynamically changing the interconnections in dependency of the modules connected to the ports. Both works, however, did not investigate how traffic prediction could improve the reconfiguration of the network.

Chen et al. [9] used a fuzzy based predictive traffic model to avoid congestion at high utilization while maintaining high quality of service in ATM networks. This prediction model was only applied to ATM networks. Pang et al. [10] used a fuzzy traffic predictor and also applied it to ATM traffic management. Results have been presented only for one-step prediction in contrast to our model which predicts several time steps. Otto and Schunk [11] applied fuzzy logic successfully to load forecasting for electric utilities. They did not apply it to other problems, however. Ogras and Marculescu [12] proposed a flow control algorithm to predict switch-to-switch traffic. This prediction is decentralized and based on the information the routers receive directly from their neighbors. From the prediction the number of packets injected in the network is controlled. Brand et al. [13] presented a congestion control strategy based on a Model Predictive Controller which controls the offered load. This method requires that routing is not dynamic, however, in contrast to our model.

The approach presented in this paper differs from and improves upon the ones mentioned above as follows. First, our approach uses a fuzzy based algorithm while previous approaches use a table-driven predictor or flow control algorithm. Second, our method predicts several future time steps which allows to avoid congestion or low utilization in a more flexible way. For example, reconfiguration of a network takes some time and is gainful only when the sum of the reconfiguration time and message transfer time after the reconfiguration is shorter than the transfer time without reconfiguration. It is therefore necessary to predict several time steps ahead to be more flexible for reconfiguration.

III. MOTIVATIONAL EXAMPLE

Communications that take place at the same time is the reason for blocking in the network. Assume, for example, a mesh NoC topology with 5×5, nodes as depicted in Figure 1. In both figures it is illustrated that node $(2, 0)$ communicates with node $(0, 4)$ (indicated by solid lines). With dimension-order (xy) routing the communication is established by first routing the message horizontally followed by routing it vertically. Additional messages that are sent simultaneously and need to cross the same links as the first message cannot reach their destination and a congestion occurs. Such an example is shown in Figure 1(a), where an additional message transfer should be established between nodes $(2, 1)$ and $(3, 3)$ (indicated by dotted line) as well as the nodes $(4, 4)$ and $(1, 4)$ (indicated by dashed line). These communication cannot

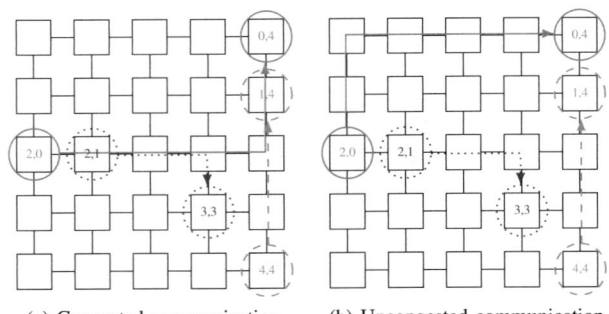

(a) Congested communication   (b) Uncongested communication

Fig. 1.   Reducing congestion by rerouting communications

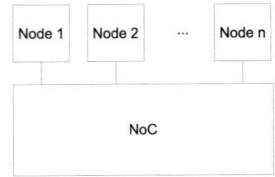

Fig. 2.   System as a black box

take place until the first communication releases the switching elements.

With traffic prediction it could be known a priori that the above mentioned nodes want to communicate. With this knowledge a different routing decision could be taken. Alternative routing paths are shown in Figure 1(b). The first communication between nodes $(2, 0)$ and $(0, 4)$ (indicated by solid line) could be realized by dimension-order (yx) routing which first routes the message vertically and then horizontally. With this new routing decision the other nodes $(2, 1)$ and $(3, 3)$ (indicated by dotted line) as well as $(4, 4)$ and $(1, 4)$ (indicated by dashed line) can communicate in parallel. This example illustrates the advantages of traffic prediction to realize blocking free communications. We remark that deadlocks could arise due to the new routing decision, but this is not the main focus of this work, since it can be solved using other techniques such as virtual channels [14].

IV. END-TO-END TRAFFIC PREDICTION

Normally it is important to know the specific NoC topology to be able to analyze it. In order to generalize our method we do not consider the specific network topology. Instead, our goal is to predict end-to-end communication. This means that we do not consider the switching elements between the nodes. It is also irrelevant which type of components (e.g. core, memory, I/O) is connected to the NoC. Every component is simply seen as a node. The NoC is considered as black box to which several node are connected.

The structure of the model is depicted in Figure 2. For the communication between nodes it is important to know which nodes want to exchange information between them and when. Therefore the point of time at which communication takes places and the amount of data that is transmitted are needed.

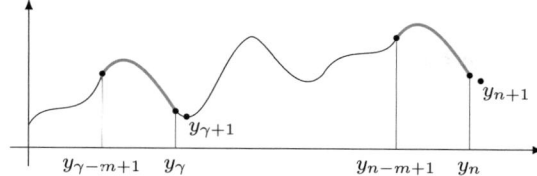

Fig. 3. Search for similar pattern in the history

With these assumptions the problem of predicting traffic in NoCs is similar to predicting a time series.

V. FUZZY BASED TRAFFIC PREDICTOR

The proposed traffic predictor is based on [11] and uses fuzzy logic, introduced by Zadeh in 1965 [15]. Fuzzy logic has no strict assignment of elements to sets like binary logic. Instead, every element has a *degree* of membership to a set. This degree is represented by a value between 0 and 1. To be able to apply fuzzy logic to a specific problem such as the prediction of a time series, a fuzzy system must be constructed. The construction consists of three steps:

1) **Fuzzyfication**: In this step the degree of membership of the input values is assigned to fuzzy sets. The degree of membership is given by $\mu : X \rightarrow [0,1]$, where X is the set of input values. So every input value is mapped to a value between 0 and 1.
2) **Fuzzy-Inference**: In this step the output values from the membership function are linked with several different functions to generate an output set.
3) **De-Fuzzyfication**: In this step a numerical output value is generated from the output set.

The above mentioned steps are used to predict a time series. To do so several time steps from the past are needed. The idea behind the algorithm is to consider the latest m $(m < n)$ data points from the time series $Y = (y_0, y_1, \cdots, y_n)$ and then search for some similar patterns in the past. We refer to m as the *pattern length*. The time series Y has $n+1$ data points. To determine similarity between patterns, fuzzy logic is used. If there are some similar patterns in the past, the algorithm forecasts the next step by interpreting these patterns. This method is depicted in Figure 3. The last data points between (y_n) and (y_{n-m+1}) are compared with pattern from the history communication. If there is a pattern of pattern length m in the past that is very similar to the latest one, like the pattern between (y_γ) and $(y_{\gamma-m+1})$, the algorithm predicts, that the next future point (y_{n+1}) is also very similar to the point that follows the past pattern $(y_{\gamma+1})$. The latest m data points correspond to a sub vector $Y[n-m+1, n] = (y_{n-m+1}, \cdots, y_{n-1}, y_n)$ and this vector is used as a window. That window vector is subtracted iteratively from the past data points, so that in total $j = n - m + 1$ difference vectors $D^{(n-m-i)} = (d_0^{(n-m-i)}, d_1^{(n-m-i)}, \cdots, d_{m-1}^{(n-m-i)})$

are obtained $(i \in [0, n-m])$, where $D^{(n-m-i)}$ is given by

$$D^{(n-m-i)} = Y[n-m-i, n-1-i] \quad (1)$$
$$- Y[n-m+1, n].$$

The superscripts indicate the different difference vectors. All elements of the calculated difference vectors are mapped using the membership function $\mu : X \rightarrow [0,1]$ to a value between 0 and 1 which shows the similarity to the original data points from the past. In this work the triangular function, given by

$$\mu(x) = \begin{cases} 1 - \left|\frac{x}{w}\right|, & \text{if } |x| < |w| \\ 0, & \text{otherwise} \end{cases} \quad (2)$$

is used as membership function. In this expression w is the width of the membership function. The width is a degree of how much the latest data points differs from those in the past and can be set by the user. If the difference is too high, the membership function generates the output value 0, which means there is no similarity. Applying the membership function is the first step (fuzzyfication) from the fuzzy system. All j difference vectors are now weighted based on to their similarity. This is done by multiplying all memberships of all elements of a difference vector, as given by the following equation

$$\beta^{(n-m-i)} = \prod_{k=0}^{m-1} \mu\left(d_k^{(n-m-i)}\right). \quad (3)$$

In this equation $d_k^{(n-m-i)}$ is element k of difference vector $D^{(n-m-i)}$. So every difference vector is now reduced to a scalar value which reflects the similarity of the patterns from the past to the last m data points. This step corresponds to the fuzzy-inference step.

From these weights we calculate the next future data point by performing a weighted sum of all past data points. This is done by the following equation

$$y_{n+1} = \frac{\sum_{\gamma=0}^{n-m} \beta^{(n-m-\gamma)} \cdot y_{n-\gamma}}{\sum_{\gamma=0}^{n-m} \beta^{(n-m-\gamma)}}. \quad (4)$$

This step corresponds to de-fuzzyfication.

The steps explained above predict the next future data point. To predict several data points, the algorithm can be reapplied including the predicted data point.

To predict future data points, we need several data points from the past. The more data points are available, the higher the possibility is to find a very similar pattern in the past and increase the accuracy of the algorithm. The disadvantage of using all data points from the past is that the calculation time and memory requirements increase. So a trade-off must be made between the number of considered data points and the accuracy of the algorithm. This trade-off depends on how often some communication patterns repeat. If some communication patterns repeat very often, fewer data points are needed than with less repetitive patterns. The effect of the history length as well as the pattern length m on the accuracy of the proposed algorithm is investigated in Section VI.

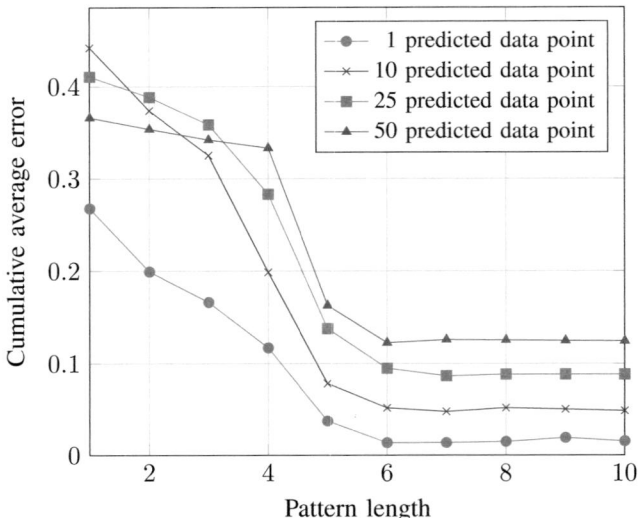

Fig. 4. Cumulative average error as a function of the pattern length

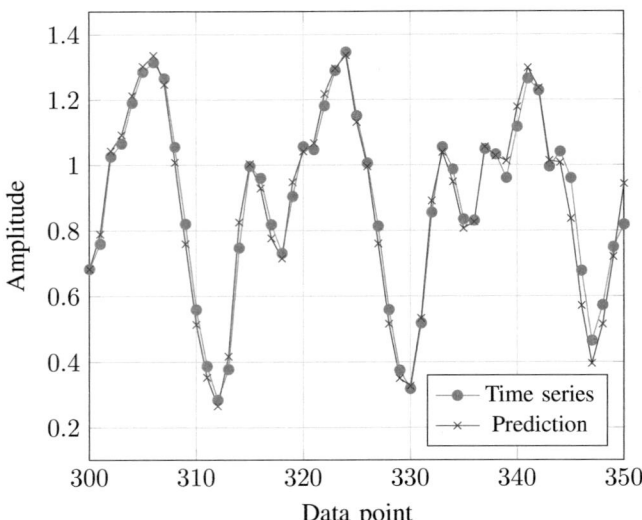

Fig. 5. Generated and predicted data points (history length is 300)

VI. EXPERIMENTAL RESULTS AND ANALYSIS

In this section experimental results are provided using two types of inputs. First, a chaotic time series will be used as input to the proposed algorithm. Thereafter, traces from a real MPI application will be used.

A. Mackey-Glass

First the proposed algorithm is tested with a chaotic time series given by the Mackey-Glass differential equation [16]:

$$\frac{dx}{dt} = \beta \cdot \frac{x_\tau}{1 + x_\tau{}^n} - \gamma \cdot x. \tag{5}$$

To generate a chaotic time series from this equation, the parameters are set as follows: $\beta = 0.2$, $\gamma = 0.1$, and $n = 10$. In this equation x_τ represents the value of the variable x at time $(t-\tau)$. The first 600 data points are calculated by solving the differential equation.

The pattern length m is an important parameter for the accuracy of the proposed algorithm. Therefore, the impact of the pattern length on the accuracy of the algorithm is investigated first. To perform this investigation the pattern length varied from 1 to 10 and the history length is set to 300. Furthermore, the algorithm is used to predict different numbers of data points. For every number of predicted data points the cumulative average error is calculated. The cumulative average error after n data points is the average error of the first n data points. Figure 4 depicts the cumulative average error as a function of the pattern length. The results show that the cumulative average error decreases when the pattern length is increased up to a length of 7. Therefore, all further investigations with the Mackey-Glass time series, the pattern length m is set to 7.

Figure 5 compares the predicted data points to the data points generated by Equation (5) for up to 50 predicted data points. The history length is set to 300. Thus the algorithm only considers the last 300 data points to make a prediction. The

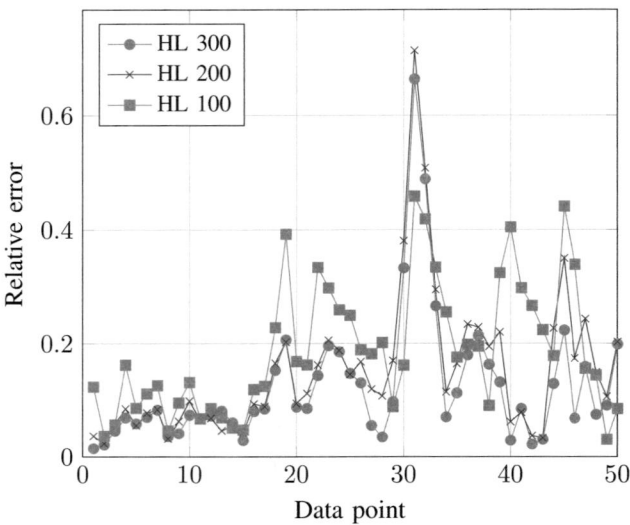

Fig. 6. Average error for 50 predicted data points with different history lengths (HL)

width w of the membership function, Equation (2), is set to 0.3. The predicted data points differs only slightly from the generated data points. The average error in Figure 5 is less than 4.5%.

The history length is another important parameter for the accuracy of the proposed algorithm. Therefore the impact of the history length on the accuracy of the algorithm is investigated in more detail. To perform this investigation, the starting point for the prediction is set to four different values, and from there on 50 data points are predicted. Afterwards the average error for every predicted point is calculated. This experiment is performed for different history lengths. Figure 6 depicts the average error for each predicted data point and Figure 7 depicts the cumulative average error after a certain number of data points have been predicted. The cumulative

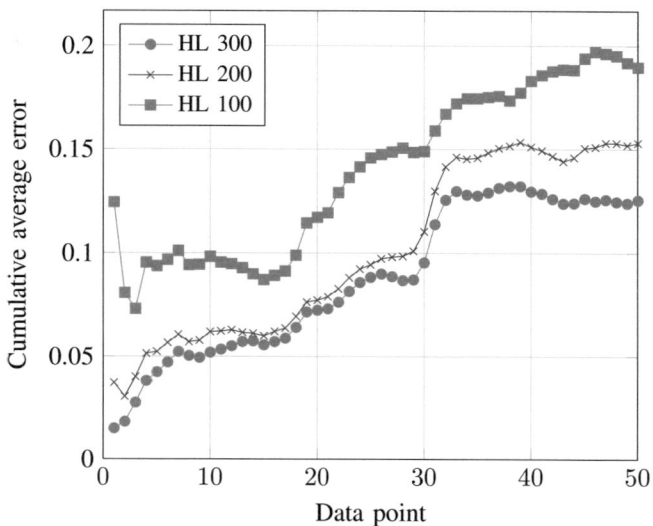

Fig. 7. Cumulative average error for different history lengths (HL)

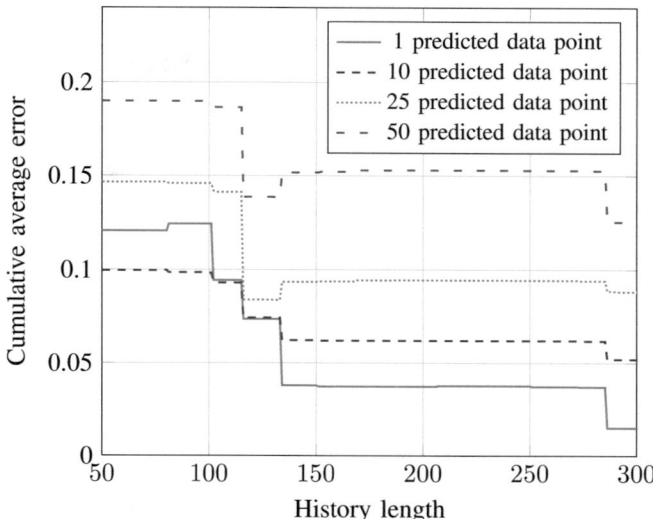

Fig. 8. Cumulative average error as a function of the history length

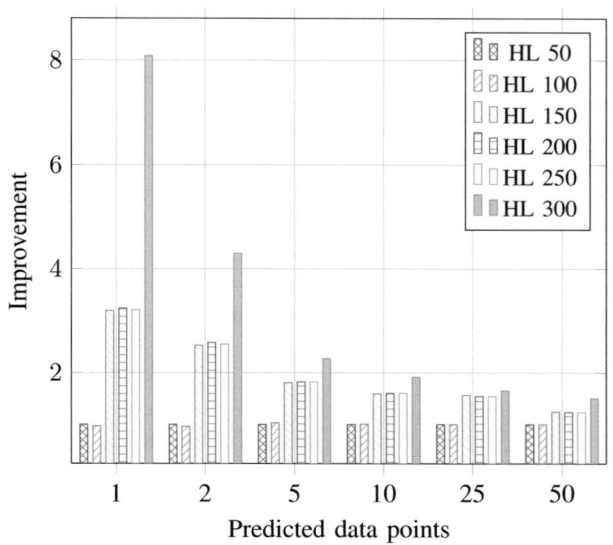

Fig. 9. Prediction accuracy normalized to the prediction accuracy obtained for a history length (HL) of 50 for different numbers of predicted data points.

average error after n data points is the average error of the first n data points in Figure 6. In both Figure 6 and Figure 7, different history lengths of 100, 200 and 300 have been used. These results show that the algorithm has the ability to predict up to 10 data points with high accuracy (5.2% error) for a chaotic time series with a history depth of 300. The high accuracy is achieved because of the continuous data points. The results also shows that the error increases when the history length is reduced. When 10 future data points need to be predicted the cumulative average error increases to 6.2% for a history length of 200, and to 9.8% for a history length of 100. There is a direct dependence between the first predicted values and the error propagation for succeeding data points. Predicted data points are used for the prediction of the succeeding data point. The error accumulates from data point to data point so error propagation happens. With a longer history lengths the error for the first predicted value is smaller and only a minor error propagation takes places. The algorithm miss predicts a peak in step 31 for all history lengths, which results in an error peak depicted in Figure 6.

Figure 8 depicts the cumulative average error as a function of the history length. The history length is varied from 50 to 300. The four lines correspond to different number of predicted data points (1, 10, 25, 50). The figure shows that the first accuracy improvement occurs when the history length is between 100 and 150. Afterwards the history length has no considerable influence on the accuracy of the predicted data points up to a history length of around 280. Another improvement of the prediction accuracy takes place beyond a history length of 280. It can be seen that for 25 and 50 predicted data points, using a history length of e.g. 125 yields better predictions than using longer history lengths. We cannot fully explain this behavior, but expect this is due to the "period" of the chaotic time series. Figure 9 depicts normalized prediction accuracy for different history lengths. The accuracy is normalized with respect to

the shortest considered history length (50). This figure shows that the history length has a huge impact on the prediction accuracy. When one data point is predicted, the accuracy is improved by a factor of 8 when the history length is increased for 50 to 300. However, the impact of the history length decreases when the number of predicted data points increases. When 50 data points are predicted, the improvement is reduced to a factor of 1.5.

B. MPI Application

1) Traffic Trace: To validate the proposed algorithm on real traffic patterns, traffic traces from real applications are needed. To generate these traces the application Meep [17] is used. Meep is a free finite-difference time-domain (FDTD) simulation software package developed at MIT to model

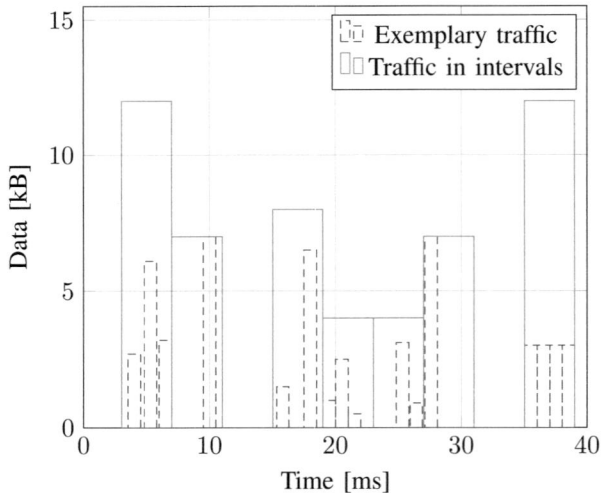

Fig. 10. Non-equidistant MPI communication patterns become equidistant

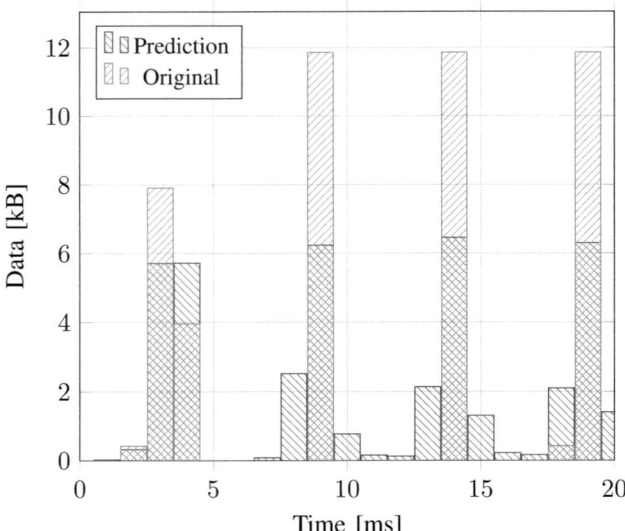

Fig. 11. Prediction of MPI communications (first behavior)

electromagnetic systems. The program has the ability to to parallelize a problem with the Message Passing Interface (MPI) which is used for the communication between processes. For our purpose Meep is used with OpenMPI [18].

Every communication is recorded using the MPItrace tool [19]. This tool traces the basic activities in an MPI program and generates a Paraver [20] trace file. This trace file includes information about thread states and communication. For our purpose only the communication information between MPI processes is relevant. Therefore a short script has been implemented that separates the communication information from the rest. A drawback of the MPItrace tool is, however, that the start and end time of every communication correspond to the time when the MPI functions (send and receive) are called respectively return. This calls the logical communication. It is not possible to determine when the real (physical) communication takes places. How we dealt with this problem is described in the next section.

The application Meep has been running on a server with 2 processors with 4 cores each.

2) MPI Analysis: The dashed bars in Figure 10 depicts exemplary the amount of data sent by an arbitrary core over time. The figure shows that the gap between two transferred messages and also the amount of data that is sent vary. This leads to a prediction problem with two unknown variables, since the problem is not only to predict how much data is sent but also at which time. There is a large difference between not knowing if a certain data point in time exists or to know that there is a data point whose value may be zero. This means that the time between two communications in the time domain are not equidistant, which introduces problems for the proposed algorithm. The introduced algorithm cannot deal with this problem because there are too many unknown variables. The algorithm can predict only one unknown variable over an equidistant scale, for example, the amount of data that is sent at a fixed point in time. For that reason the problem must be

reduced in order to be able to apply the proposed algorithm. To reduce this problem, time is divided into fixed sized intervals. In every time interval, the amount of data that is sent is summed up. The solid bars in Figure 10 depict the amount of data sent in each time interval. The advantage of time intervals is that now the time axis no longer has non-equidistant time steps. Therefore the above mentioned problem with two unknown variables has been reduced to a problem with one unknown, namely to predict the amount of data that will be sent. With this technique the problem that the tracing tool provides only traces with logical communication information is also reduced. It can be assumed that the physical communication will take place shortly after the logical so the assumption is made that most communications will start in the corresponding time interval, provided the size of the interval is not too short. For communications that take places at the end of a time interval it, cannot be determined if they are assigned to the correct time interval. This side effect will be neglected. The proposed algorithm should predict up to 20 prospective time intervals. The width of the membership function, Equation (2), is set to 5.5 and the pattern length m is set to 7. When predicting the MPI communication traces two behaviors have been observed, which are depicted in Figure 11 and Figure 12. The first data point numbered zero in both figures is the real one. Therefore the measured and predicted values match. The prediction starts in time interval 1. In time intervals where no bars are visible the communication volume during this interval is zero.

Both figures show the amount of data sent in each time interval. The dashed bars depict the real data and the solid bars the predicted. The first behavior is depicted in Figure 11. The time at which a communication takes places is predicted with high accuracy, but the predicted amount of data is below the actual amount. The second behavior is depicted in Figure 12. In this case the amount of transmitted data is predicted better

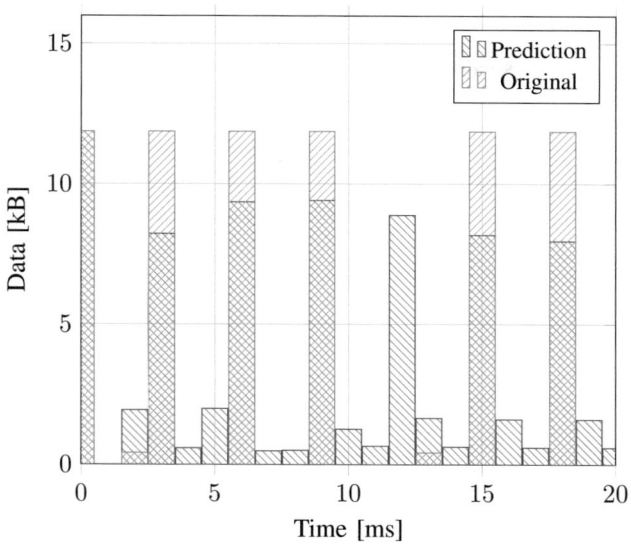

Fig. 12.   Prediction of MPI communications (second behavior)

TABLE I
ABSOLUTE AVERAGE ERROR IN KB

Steps	1	2	5	10	20
Avg. Err. (Fig. 11)	0.008	0.768	1.551	1.498	1.920
Avg. Err. (Fig. 12)	0.246	1.596	2.442	2.427	2.656

than in the case depicted in Figure 11. The algorithm also, however, predicts communication peaks where no peaks are. This can be seen in time interval 12.

Table I shows the absolute average error in kB for both figures after several predictions steps. It is not possible to present the relative error because several data points are zero which would lead to a division by zero. Table I shows that a 1-step prediction can be performed with high accuracy for both behaviors. For the first behavior also a 2-step prediction has a small error. After that the error increases but stays nearly constant up to step 10. Thereafter the error increases more and more because of error propagation.

The miss predictions for both shown behaviors arise from the relative distance between two data points in contiguous time intervals, especially when a peak communication is followed by the absence of communication or vice versa. Such jumps mislead the proposed algorithm so that a wrong estimation is produced. The communication patterns from the history are weighted incorrectly so an error arises which influences coming data points.

To interpret the presented results it must be taken into account that only static simulations are performed. Data points that occur far into the future are predicted with previously predicted values. That means that no new data points are taken into account so that the error propagates. In a real system the time goes on and new data points are produced and so the history is updated. In that case more real data points could be used to predict the next data points, which would lead to slower error

propagation. This is identical to a prediction with few future time intervals. Moreover, the size of the time intervals must also be taken into account. The size of a time interval is set by the user so that one interval could correspond to many clock cycles. Based on the problem one or two predicted intervals could be sufficient.

VII. CONCLUSIONS AND FUTURE WORK

In this paper a model has been proposed to predict end-to-end traffic in NoC-based multiprocessor systems. The model predicts end-to-end communication, so intermediate switching elements are not considered. A fuzzy based algorithm is employed that searches for similar traffic patterns in the history to predict prospective data points. The prediction is performed for time intervals. Experimental results have been provided for a chaotic time series as well as real traffic patterns obtained by tracing an MPI application on a multiprocessor system. The accuracy of the prediction depends mainly on the behavior the traffic patterns that should be predicted. Chaotic patterns with continuous behavior can be predicted with high accuracy for up to 10 data points. Traffic patterns that are non-continuous, jumping from high communication volume to zero communication or vice versa, can also be predicted accurately, but only up to two steps ahead. Accurately predicting two data points can be sufficient, however, because the prediction is performed for time intervals and one interval consist of many clock cycles.

As future work, we plan to validate the proposed method on a NoC system. To do that the proposed algorithm must be integrated into a NoC simulator. This step allows us to investigate the NoC system speedup due to traffic prediction. Furthermore, this step is important to check how the prediction of future data points influences the NoC system. Also the computational complexity of the model must be analyzed and optimized in order to be able to integrate the proposed model in NoC systems. On a real NoC system, it could be validated how many time steps must be predicted in order to improve the system performance. Furthermore, the prediction accuracy of the algorithm could be improved. In particular the amount of data that is transferred could be predicted with higher accuracy, since the predicted amount is currently below the actual amount.

REFERENCES

[1] D. Geer, "Chip Makers Turn to Multicore Processors," *Computer*, vol. 38, no. 5, pp. 11 – 13, May 2005.
[2] P. Gepner and M. Kowalik, "Multi-Core Processors: New Way to Achieve High System Performance," in *Parallel Computing in Electrical Engineering, 2006. PAR ELEC 2006. International Symposium on*, 2006, pp. 9 –13.
[3] B. Ahmad, A. Erdogan, and S. Khawam, "Architecture of a Dynamically Reconfigurable NoC for Adaptive Reconfigurable MPSoC," in *Adaptive Hardware and Systems, 2006. AHS 2006. First NASA/ESA Conference on*, 2006, pp. 405 –411.
[4] A. Hansson and K. Goossens, "Trade-offs in the Configuration of a Network on Chip for Multiple Use-Cases," in *Networks-on-Chip, 2007. NOCS 2007. First International Symposium on*, May 2007, pp. 233 – 242.

[5] Y. Huang, K.-K. Chou, C.-T. King, and S.-Y. Tseng, "NTPT: On the End-to-End Traffic Prediction in the On-Chip Networks," in *Design Automation Conference (DAC), 2010 47th ACM/IEEE*, 2010, pp. 449 –452.

[6] S. Kaxiras and C. Young, "Coherence communication prediction in shared-memory multiprocessors ," in *High-Performance Computer Architecture, 2000. HPCA-6. Proceedings. Sixth International Symposium on*, 2000, pp. 156 –167.

[7] J. Duato, O. Lysne, R. Pang, and T. Pinkston, "A Theory for Deadlock-Free Dynamic Network Reconfiguration. Part I," *Parallel and Distributed Systems, IEEE Transactions on*, vol. 16, no. 5, pp. 412 – 427, May 2005.

[8] O. Lysne, T. Pinkston, and J. Duato, "A Methodology for Developing Deadlock-Free Dynamic Network Reconfiguration Processes. Part II," *Parallel and Distributed Systems, IEEE Transactions on*, vol. 16, no. 5, pp. 428 – 443, May 2005.

[9] B.-S. Chen, Y.-S. Yang, B.-K. Lee, and T.-H. Lee, "Fuzzy Adaptive Predictive Flow Control of ATM Network traffic," *Fuzzy Systems, IEEE Transactions on*, vol. 11, no. 4, pp. 568 – 581, 2003.

[10] Q. Pang, S. Cheng, and P. Zhang, "Adaptive fuzzy traffic predictor and its applications in ATM networks," in *Communications, 1998. ICC 98. Conference Record.1998 IEEE International Conference on*, vol. 3, Jun. 1998, pp. 1759 –1763 vol.3.

[11] P. Otto and T. Schunk, "Fuzzybasierte Zeitreihenvorhersage," *Automatisierungstechnik*, vol. 48, pp. 327–334, 2000, In: German.

[12] U. Y. Ogras and R. Marculescu, "Prediction-based Flow Control for Network-on-Chip Traffic," in *Proceedings of the 43rd annual Design Automation Conference*, ser. DAC '06.   New York, NY, USA: ACM, 2006, pp. 839–844. [Online]. Available: http://doi.acm.org/10.1145/1146909.1147123

[13] J. van den Brand, C. Ciordas, K. Goossens, and T. Basten, "Congestion-Controlled Best-Effort Communication for Networks-on-Chip," in *Design, Automation Test in Europe Conference Exhibition, 2007. DATE '07*, 2007, pp. 1 –6.

[14] W. Dally and C. Seitz, "Deadlock-Free Message Routing in Multiprocessor Interconnection Networks," *Computers, IEEE Transactions on*, vol. C-36, no. 5, pp. 547 –553, May 1987.

[15] L. Zadeh, "Fuzzy Sets," *Information and Control*, vol. 8, pp. 338–353, 1965.

[16] L. Glass and M. C. Mackey, "Oscillation and Chaos in Physiological Control Systems," *Science*, vol. 197, pp. 287–289, 1977.

[17] S. G. Johnson, J. D. Joannopoulos, and M. Soljai, "Meep," 2006. [Online]. Available: http://ab-initio.mit.edu/wiki/index.php/Meep

[18] E. Gabriel, G. E. Fagg, G. Bosilca, T. Angskun, J. J. Dongarra, J. M. Squyres, V. Sahay, P. Kambadur, B. Barrett, A. Lumsdaine, R. H. Castain, D. J. Daniel, R. L. Graham, and T. S. Woodall, "Open MPI: Goals, Concept, and Design of a Next Generation MPI Implementation," in *Proceedings, 11th European PVM/MPI Users' Group Meeting*, Budapest, Hungary, September 2004, pp. 97–104.

[19] H. S. Gelabert and G. L. Snchez, "MPItrace - User Guide Manual," 2010. [Online]. Available: http://www.bsc.es/plantillaA.php?cat_id=492

[20] *Paraver - Parallel Program Visualization and Analysis tool*, Version 3.1 ed., Barcelona Supercomputing Center - Centro Nacional de Supercomputacin, October 2001. [Online]. Available: http://www.bsc.es/plantillaA.php?cat_id=493

GPU Acceleration of the Assembly Process for Isogeometric Analysis

Nathan Collier
Aron Ahmadia
V. M. Calo
Applied Mathematics and Computational Science
Earth and Environmental Sciences and Engineering
King Abdullah University of Science and Technology
Thuwal, Saudi Arabia

Hyoseop Lee
Craig C. Douglas
Department of Mathematics
University of Wyoming
Laramie, Wyoming 82071-3036, USA

Abstract—**We present a method for graphics processing unit (GPU) acceleration of matrix assembly as applied to isogeometric analysis, spline-based isoparametric finite elements. We take advantage of the basis being defined on a structured grid to precompute basis functions and assemble the local contributions to the stiffness matrix on the GPU. We show how GPU resources may be utilized with minor changes to a serial code. This initial work achieves a speedup of up to 11 in the matrix assembly stage of the isogeometric finite element algorithm.**

Index Terms—**GPU, isogeometric, finite elements, matrix assembly, acceleration, CUDA**

I. INTRODUCTION

Isogeometric analysis [1] is a new method proposed in 2005, originally motivated by the desire to find a technique for solving partial differential equations which would simplify, if not eliminate the problem of converting geometric descriptions for discretizations in the engineering design process. Once a design is born inside a Computer Aided Design (CAD) program, the process to convert it to an analysis suitable form is the bottleneck of the analysis process, consuming up to 80% of this process. Isogeometric analysis aims to use CAD representations directly by using the B-spline or NURBS (Non-uniform Rational B-Spline) basis in isoparametric finite elements.

The term *isogeometric* refers to the fact that all representations of the problem have the same (iso) geometry. Refinement of a finite element space changes the geometry and requires communication to and from the original CAD description. Isogeometric analysis is capable of geometry preserving refinements, meaning that there is no need to return to the CAD description. The refinements available to isogeometric analysis are richer than in the standard finite element method (FEM). Isogeometric analysis possesses h-refinements (knot insertion), p-refinements (degree elevation) and k-refinements (degree elevation followed by knot insertion), all of which are geometry preserving.

This means that once a mesh is defined, which accurately describes the geometry, as refinements are needed the geometry does not change. The number of degrees of freedom necessary to represent the geometry accurately is, in most ap-

plications, much smaller than the one needed for representing the solution to the physical phenomena on that domain.

Isogeometric analysis is isoparametric finite elements using the Bernstein basis in place of the Lagrange basis traditionally used [2]. The Bernstein bases has been used in CAD for several decades due to several of its properties, particularly the smoothness of the basis and ability to represent conic sections in its rational form. For this reason typically NURBS are used, yet at the core they are piecewise polynomials possessing higher orders of continuity.

In addition to the geometrical benefits, the basis is also well suited to solving nonlinear and higher-order partial differential equations due to its higher-order continuity. Isogeometric analysis has successfully been applied to a number of areas including, structural vibrations, fluid-structure interaction, particularly patient-specific arterial blood flow, complex fluid flow and turbulence, shape optimization, phase field models via the Cahn-Hilliard equation, cavitation modeling, and shell analysis [3]–[10]. In addition, a book [11] has been written, detailing the method and showcasing several applications. Due to this increased interest in both engineering and scientific applications, it is important that codes which implement this method are efficient.

Although, as their name indicates, the primary role of a graphical processing unit (GPU) is to accelerate graphics rendering, computational scientists have demonstrated impressive performance and speedups over traditional scientific codes by offloading computationally intensive routines to GPUs [12]–[14]. Graphical processing units have also become increasingly popular in the solution of partial differential equations, principally via the finite difference method (for example [15], [16]). Finite difference methods map well onto GPUs due to their structured topology and low memory requirements.

Recent work has looked towards acceleration of finite element solvers via GPUs. Research has been published addressing the optimization of the sparse matrix solves [17] as well as the assembly of matrix equations in unstructured meshes [18]. In spite of their speedups in computational time, the limited memory size of a GPU restricts the problem size that can be solved on a single GPU. A GPU cluster is a possible solution

41

to tackle the limitation. In [19] we already utilized a GPU cluster as a linear solver for finite element simulation. In this paper we are concerned with the local matrix assembly of the matrix equations used in isogeometric analysis on a single GPU, which can be naturally extended into a GPU cluster. The combination of this work and the linear solve on a GPU cluster will be a forthcoming paper.

The purpose of this paper is two-fold. First, we present an algorithmic analysis of the stiffness matrix assembly process using NURBS as the basis. We present results specific to elasticity equations in three-dimensions. While the NURBS basis functions are capable of representing complex geometries, topologically each patch has a tensor product structure in the parametric domain. This fact allows for some computational efficiencies previously unutilized. Second, we present an adaptation of a publicly distributed NURBS code [20] which takes advantage of these efficiencies as well as utilizes the GPU.

II. ISOGEOMETRIC ANALYSIS

Isogeometric analysis is a Galerkin finite element method that uses B-spline basis functions. These basis functions are polynomial splines based on the Bernstein basis. A spline space is defined by first specifying a knot vector, a one-dimensional set of non-decreasing locations in parametric space. The knot vector is denoted by

$$\Xi = \{\xi_1, \xi_2, \ldots, \xi_{n+p+1}\},$$

where $\xi_i \in \mathbb{R}$ is the ith knot, p is the polynomial order, and n is the number of basis functions. The knot vector encodes the basis functions, which can be evaluated using the Cox-deBoor recursion formula, described in what follows. The zeroth order functions are defined as

$$N_{i,0}(\xi) = \begin{cases} 1 & \text{if } \xi_i \leq \xi < \xi_{i+1}, \\ 0 & \text{otherwise}, \end{cases}$$

while for $p > 0$,

$$N_{i,p}(\xi) = \frac{\xi - \xi_i}{\xi_{i+p} - \xi_i} N_{i,p-1}(\xi) + \frac{\xi_{i+p+1} - \xi}{\xi_{i+p+1} - \xi_{i+1}} N_{i+1,p-1}(\xi).$$

Sample basis functions can be seen in Fig. 1. Higher orders of continuity have the effect of extending the support of the basis functions beyond their typical single element support.

A. Why Rationals?

Rational B-splines (commonly referred to as NURBS) are used because low degree of freedom polynomial spaces poorly approximate conic sections. This can be demonstrated by considering a quadratic Bernstein representation of a quarter circle, shown in Fig. 2(a). The corresponding polynomial basis is shown below in Fig. 2(c). Note that to maintain the tangency at the endpoints, the middle control point must be located in the corner of the inscribed square. So each basis is weighted (Fig. 2(d)) to precisely match the circle (Fig. 2(b)). This enables a low-degree-of-freedom, exact representation of conic sections, common in engineering design applications.

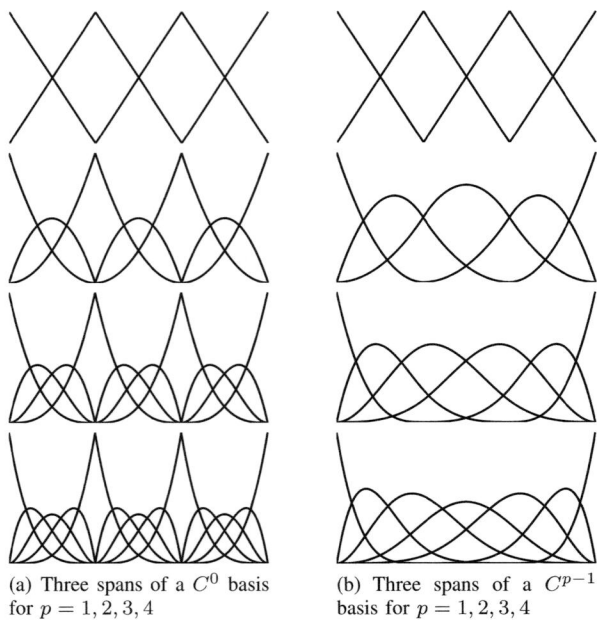

(a) Three spans of a C^0 basis for $p = 1, 2, 3, 4$

(b) Three spans of a C^{p-1} basis for $p = 1, 2, 3, 4$

Fig. 1.   Examples of B-spline basis functions

In multi-dimensions the rational basis functions, R_i^p, can be formed directly from the polynomial counterparts, $N_{i,p}$, by weighting each basis, w_i, and then dividing by the sum of all functions to maintain the partition of unity property. Here p refers to the polynomial order and i indexes the basis,

$$R_i^p(\xi) = \frac{N_{i,p}(\xi) w_i}{\sum_{\hat{i}} N_{\hat{i},p}(\xi) w_{\hat{i}}}.$$

The polynomial basis functions are formed by tensor product and the rationals are formed subsequently. For example in three-dimensions

$$R_{i,j,k}^{p,q,r}(\xi,\eta,\zeta) = \frac{N_{i,p}(\xi) M_{j,q}(\eta) L_{k,r}(\zeta) w_{i,j,k}}{\sum_{\hat{i}} \sum_{\hat{j}} \sum_{\hat{k}} N_{\hat{i},p}(\xi) M_{\hat{j},q}(\eta) L_{\hat{k},r}(\zeta) w_{i,j,k}},$$

where N, M, L are the one dimensional basis functions, p, q, r denote polynomial order in each direction and i, j, k index the basis. Note that this is not a tensor product structure since the denominator couples all directions, thus $R_{i,j,k}^{p,q,r}$ cannot be written as the product of three functions where each depends on a single parametric direction.

B. Elasticity

We focus on the acceleration of stiffness matrix formation using NURBS basis functions, particularly we address the case of linear elasticity. The elasticity equations are derived in many references, such as [11]. The strong form is to find $u_i : \bar{\Omega} \to \mathbb{R}$ given that $f_i : \Omega \to \mathbb{R}$, $g_i : \Gamma_{D_i} \to \mathbb{R}$, and $h_i : \Gamma_{N_i} \to \mathbb{R}$ such that,

$$\sigma_{ij,j} + f_i = 0 \text{ in } \Omega,$$
$$u_i = g_i \text{ on } \Gamma_{D_i},$$
$$\sigma_{ij} n_i = h_i \text{ on } \Gamma_{N_i},$$

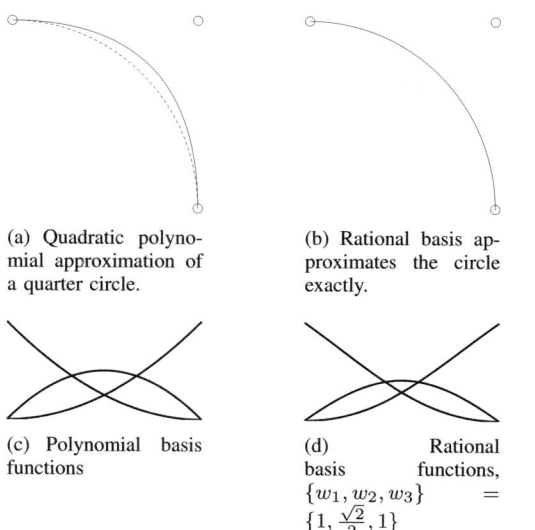

(a) Quadratic polynomial approximation of a quarter circle.

(b) Rational basis approximates the circle exactly.

(c) Polynomial basis functions

(d) Rational basis functions, $\{w_1, w_2, w_3\} = \{1, \frac{\sqrt{2}}{2}, 1\}$

Fig. 2. Rational basis functions approximate conic sections, such as circles, exactly. The circle appears as dashed line, control points appear as small circles.

where the stress, σ_{ij}, is related to the symmetric part of the displacement gradient, $u_{i,j}$, by a linear constituitive law, known as generalized Hooke's law,

$$\sigma_{ij} = c_{ijkl}\epsilon_{kl},$$

with

$$\epsilon_{kl} = \frac{1}{2}\left(u_{i,j} + u_{j,i}\right),$$

and

$$c_{ijkl} = \lambda\delta_{ij}\delta_{kl} + \mu\left(\delta_{ik}\delta_{jl} + \delta_{il}\delta_{jk}\right),$$

where λ and μ are the so-called Lamé constants, and δ_{ij} is the Kronecker delta, defined as 1 if $i = j$ and 0 otherwise.

Assuming the pointwise satisfaction of the constitutive relation, the weak form of the elasticity equations is stated as: find $u_i \in S_i$ which satisfies the Dirichlet condition $u_i = g_i$ on Γ_{D_i} such that for all $w_i \in V_i$ which satisfy $w_i = 0$ on Γ_{D_i}

$$\int_\Omega w_{(i,j)}\sigma_{ij}d\Omega = \int_\Omega w_i f_i d\Omega + \sum_{i=1}^d \left(\int_{\Gamma_{N_i}} w_i h_i d\Gamma\right),$$

where u_i denotes the displacement vector components, $u_{i,j}$ denotes the the derivative of u_i in the direction of x_j, σ_{ij} and ϵ_{ij} are the components of the Cauchy stress and small strain tensors, respectively, and c_{ijkl} denotes the component of the elasticity tensor. The reader is referred to section 4.1 of [11] for more details on the formation of matrix equations from this weak form.

III. ALGORITHM

In this section we describe the methods used to accelerate the assembly process of the stiffness matrix in finite element analysis. Note that while the work here is specific to linear elasticity, most of the insights apply to other weak forms as well. We present the algorithmic changes relative to those presented in [11]. For reference the algorithm for a multi-patch isogeometric finite element code is presented here and designated Alg. 1.

Algorithm 1 Original Isogeometric Analysis

1: Read global input data
2: Build connectivities and allocate global array
3: $K = 0$ and $F = 0$
4: **for all** patches in mesh **do**
5:     Read patch input data
6:     **for all** elements in current patch **do**
7:         $K_e = 0$ and $F_e = 0$
8:         **for all** quadrature points **do**
9:             Evaluate basis functions and derivatives
10:           Add contributions to K_e and F_e
11:         **end for**
12:         Assemble $K \leftarrow K_e$ and $F \leftarrow F_e$
13:     **end for**
14: **end for**
15: Solve $Kd = F$
16: Write output data

We profiled the reference code using input files representing a statically loaded cylinder by specifying an internal pressure. The NURBS basis exactly represents the cyliner geometry at all levels of the discretization. While cylinder problems can be analyzed using standard finite elements, doing so while exactly representing the geometry in an isoparametric framework is unique to isogeometric analysis.

To solve the system, we use a sparse conjugate gradient solver with the zero tolerance set to 10^{-8}. While the basis function routine was suspected to be a major cost of the simulation, particularly for higher p, the profile shows that the computation represents a small portion of the overall routine. We examined each routine, counting the floating point operations (FLOPS) and the memory accesses. The algorithmic intensity is the measure of the ratio of these quantities. Thus, routines with a high intensity perform more FLOPS per data access and stand to benefit more from parallelization. The algorithmic intensity was highest (0.7 and higher) in the routine which computes the local stiffness matrices. We expect this routine to achieve decent acceleration by mapping it to the GPU.

A. Precomputation of Basis Functions

The basis function computation on the GPU was avoided by a reorganization of the code to take advantage of the structured nature of tensor product splines and precompute the one-dimensional basis functions. This is not typically done as the memory to store this information grows quickly. However, NURBS-based isogeometric meshes are structured grids, not unlike finite differences. This structure enables the reuse of the same basis functions in many elements, which reduces storage requirements and removes the need to compute the basis functions on the GPU. The precomputation slightly economizes (1% speedup for matrix assembly for elasticity) the stiffness matrix assembly process, and requires a small change to the original algorithm, described in Alg. 2. This unexpected and marginal efficiency is due to the comparitively more expensive local stiffness matrix computations. In other equations were the local stiffness contributions are less intense, such as in the Laplace equation, precomputation of the basis functions can speedup matrix assembly by as much as 5%.

Algorithm 2 Isogeometric Analysis: precomputation of basis functions

1: Read global input data
2: Build connectivities and allocate global array
3: $K = 0$ and $F = 0$
4: **for all** patches in mesh **do**
5:      Read patch input data
6:      Precompute 1D basis functions   ▷ new
7:      **for all** elements in current patch **do**
8:          $K_e = 0$ and $F_e = 0$
9:          **for all** quadrature points **do**
10:             Evaluate 3D basis from 1D values   ▷ new
11:             Add contributions to K_e and F_e
12:         **end for**
13:         Assemble $K \leftarrow K_e$ and $F \leftarrow F_e$
14:     **end for**
15: **end for**
16: Solve $Kd = F$
17: Write output data

B. GPU Implementation

The strategy used here is that we compute the local stiffness matrix and load vector (K_e and F_e) on the GPU and then transfer them back to the CPU for global assembly and solution. Alg. 3 provides a schematic for how this is accomplished. We copy the precomputed 1D basis functions, the rational weights, connectivity information, and geometric information to the GPU.

Algorithm 3 Isogeometric Analysis: GPU enhanced

1: Read global input data
2: Build connectivities and allocate global array
3: $K = 0$ and $F = 0$
4: **for all** patches in mesh **do**
5:      Read patch input data
6:      Precompute 1D basis functions and derivatives
7:      **procedure** MOVE TO GPU
8:          Compute 3D basis   ▷ GPU
9:          Add contributions to K_e and F_e ▷ GPU
10:     **end procedure**
11:     Copy all K_e and F_e to the CPU
12: **end for**
13: Assemble $K \leftarrow K_e$ and $F \leftarrow F_e$
14: Solve $Kd = F$
15: Write output data

The GPU kernel launches, assigning a block for each element where each thread in the blocks is in charge of a single Gauss point. The kernel is then responsible for first, computing the three-dimensional rational basis, the isoparametric mapping and its inverse, and the basis derivatives modified by this inverse mapping. Second, the local stiffness matrix is computed for the linear-elastic weak form. Finally the local load vector is assembled. These operations are safe because the computation is independent for each Gauss point.

The implementation of the each thread is a simple porting from the original code, but the memory access pattern of the thread should be considered carefully for the sake of optimization. First of all, the variables that are accessed simultaneously by continuous threads are indexed to be coalesced into a single memory transaction. The coalesced memory access enables an efficient global memory bandwidth, and thus it plays the most important role in terms of optimization. In particular, the local stiffness matrix is stored with threadID-based indexing to achieve the coalescent memory access. The number of local variables is another consideration for efficient memory management. Local variables declared inside kernel functions are stored either on the global memory or on the register. Though the CUDA compiler determines the storage, basically the variables above the limit of registers spill to the global memory, and it can cause a serious decrease in performance. We modified the original code in order to shrink the number of local variables by removing redundant storage and computations of the original code

The last two operations of the kernel involve a summation of each thread's contribution to the matrix and the load vector and thus require reductions. The reduction over Gauss points is achieved through the shared memory on the GPU. Naive implementation of the reduction results in a considerable performance loss. The possible reasons of the loss include instruction bottleneck, bank conflict, and variable addressing. The details of the optimization strategy can be found in [21], [22]

Subsequently, the local contributions are copied back to the CPU and assembled into the global matrix. While on the GPU, each local matrix is computed ignoring Dirichlet boundary conditions. The Dirichlet boundary conditions are incorporated at the global assembly stage on the CPU.

IV. NUMERICAL RESULTS

This strategy was implemented and run on a NVIDIA Tesla C1060 with the NVIDIA CUDA compiler (release 3.2, V0.2.1221). In the result table, meshes are detailed by their polynomial order, p, the number of elements in the cardinal directions, N_x, N_y, and N_z, as well as the total number of degrees of freedom, N_{dof}. The execution times are measured excluding the time for data transfer between the CPU and the GPU. The emphasis of isogeometric analysis is that while the discretizations vary in polynomial order and number of elements, all exactly represent the cylinder geometry. Tab. I shows up to a 11-fold speedup compared to the publicly distributed implementation on a single core of the CPU (an

TABLE I
TIME COMPARISON FOR STIFFNESS MATRIX ASSEMBLY.

	Elements				(Time in *sec.*)		
p	N_x	N_y	N_z	N_{dof}	CPU	GPU	Speedup
2	32	16	8	4096	6.19	0.58	10.7
2	32	16	16	8192	12.40	1.16	10.7
2	64	16	16	16384	49.43	4.60	10.7
3	16	16	8	2048	14.85	1.56	9.5
3	32	16	8	4096	29.70	3.11	9.5
3	32	16	16	8192	59.35	6.22	9.5
4	8	8	8	512	26.27	3.10	8.5
4	16	8	8	1024	52.55	6.06	8.7
4	16	16	8	2048	105.47	12.08	8.7

Intel Xeon E5405 2.00GHz). In order to maximize the thread occupancy we split the computation of one element into two blocks only for $p = 4$. Note that the relatively low speedup for $p = 4$ is caused by a higher local memory requirement and the non-divisible number of Gauss points (5^3) by the size of half-warp (16) which loses the perfomance from the reduction.

V. CONCLUSION

We introduced isogeometric analysis in the context of linear elasticity. We described algorithmic changes that must take place in an isogeometric code to benefit from the GPU. We detailed our approach and presented numerical results which show decent speedups on a series of discretizations representing both p- and h-refinements. The approach is valuable beyond linear elasticity, only the GPU code which assembles the local stiffness matrix and load vector must be changed.

We believe that the there is a lot to be gained by fully assembling the global matrix on the GPU. Isogeometric local stiffness matrices overlap each other to greater extent than conventional finite element analysis due to higher continuity in the basis. This means that a large savings in the amount of memory can be realized by directly assembling local contributions to the global matrix. This also complicates the code because additional race conditions must be avoided. Once the global assembly is performed on the GPU we plan to also solve the system there using a sparse iterative method.

ACKNOWLEDGMENTS

This research was supported in part by NSF grants 1018072 and 1018079 and Award No. KUS-C1-016-04, made by King Abdullah University of Science and Technology (KAUST).

REFERENCES

[1] T. J. R. Hughes, J. Cottrell, and Y. Bazilevs, "Isogeometric analysis: CAD, finite elements, NURBS, exact geometry and mesh refinement," *Computer Methods in Applied Mechanics and Engineering*, vol. 194, pp. 4135–4195, 2005.

[2] M. J. Borden, M. A. Scott, J. A. Evans, and T. J. R. Hughes, "Isogeometric finite element data structures based on Bézier extraction of NURBS," *International Journal for Numerical Methods in Engineering*, 2010.

[3] Y. Bazilevs, V. M. Calo, Y. Zhang, and T. J. R. Hughes, "Isogeometric fluid-structure interaction analysis with applications to arterial blood flow," *Computational Mechanics*, vol. 38, p. 310, 2006.

[4] Y. Bazilevs, V. M. Calo, T. J. R. Hughes, and Y. Zhang, "Isogeometric fluid-structure interaction: theory, algorithms, and computations," *Computational Mechanics*, vol. 43, pp. 3–37, 2008.

[5] J. Cottrell, A. Reali, Y. Bazilevs, and T. J. R. Hughes, "Isogeometric analysis of structural vibrations." *Computer Methods in Applied Mechanics and Engineering*, vol. 195, no. 41-43, p. 5257, 2006.

[6] H. Gomez, V. M. Calo, Y. Bazilevs, and T. J. R. Hughes, "Isogeometric analysis of the Cahn-Hilliard phase-field model," *Computer Methods in Applied Mechanics and Engineering*, vol. 197, no. 49-50, pp. 4333–4352, 2008.

[7] H. Gomez, T. J. R. Hughes, X. Nogueira, and V. M. Calo, "Isogeometric analysis of the isothermal Navier-Stokes-Korteweg equations," *Computer Methods in Applied Mechanics and Engineering*, vol. 199, p. 1828, 2010.

[8] L. Dedè, T. J. R. Hughes, S. Lipton, and V. M. Calo, "Structural topology optimization with isogeometric analysis in a phase field approach," in *USNCTAM2010, 16th US National Congree of Theoretical and Applied Mechanics*, 2010.

[9] W. A. Wall, M. A. Frenzel, and C. Cyron, "Isogeometric structural shape optimization," *Computer Methods in Applied Mechanics and Engineering*, vol. 197, no. 33-40, pp. 2976 – 2988, 2008.

[10] Y. Zhang, Y. Bazilevs, S. Goswami, C. L. Bajaj, and T. J. R. Hughes, "Patient-specific vascular NURBS modeling for isogeometric analysis of blood flow," *Computer Methods in Applied Mechanics and Engineering*, vol. 196, no. 29-30, pp. 2943 – 2959, 2007.

[11] J. A. Cottrell, T. J. R. Hughes, and Y. Bazilevs, *Isogeometric Analysis: Toward Unification of CAD and FEA*. John Wiley and Sons, 2009.

[12] D. Komatitsch, D. Michéa, and G. Erlebacher, "Porting a high-order finite-element earthquake modeling application to NVIDIA graphics cards using CUDA," *Journal of Parallel and Distributed Computing*, vol. 69, no. 5, pp. 451–460, 2009.

[13] A. Nukada, Y. Ogata, T. Endo, and S. Matsuoka, "Bandwidth intensive 3-D FFT kernel for GPUs using CUDA," *Conference on High Performance Networking and Computing*, 2008.

[14] S. Ryoo, C. I. Rodrigues, S. S. Baghsorkhi, S. S. Stone, D. B. Kirk, and W. W. Hwu, "Optimization principles and application performance evaluation of a multithreaded GPU using CUDA," in *Proceedings of the 13th ACM SIGPLAN Symposium on Principles and practice of parallel programming*. ACM, 2008, pp. 73–82.

[15] S. Krakiwsky, L. Turner, and M. Okoniewski, "Acceleration of finite-difference time-domain (FDTD) using graphics processor units (GPU)," vol. 2, jun. 2004, pp. 1033–1036.

[16] P. Micikevicius, "3d finite difference computation on GPUs using CUDA," in *GPGPU-2: Proceedings of 2nd Workshop on General Purpose Processing on Graphics Processing Units*. New York, NY, USA: ACM, 2009, pp. 79–84.

[17] J. Bolz, I. Farmer, E. Grinspun, and P. Schröoder, "Sparse matrix solvers on the GPU: conjugate gradients and multigrid," *ACM Trans. Graph.*, vol. 22, pp. 917–924, July 2003.

[18] C. Cecka, A. J. Lew, and E. Darve, "Assembly of finite element methods on graphics processors," *International Journal for Numerical Methods in Engineering*, 2010.

[19] C. C. Douglas, H. Lee, G. Haase, M. Liebmann, V. Calo, and N. Collier, "Parallel algebraic multigrid method with GP-GPU hardware acceleration," 2010, submitted.

[20] "NURBS code," http://users.ices.utexas.edu/ evans/isogeometric/nurbs.zip, jan 2011.

[21] M. Harris, "Optimizaing parallel redcution in CUDA," White paper, NVIDIA Developer Technology, available online. [Online]. Available: http://http://developer.nvidia.com

[22] M. Harris, S. Sengupta, and J. D. Owens, "Parallel Prefix Sum (Scan) with CUDA," in *GPU Gems 3*, H. Nguyen, Ed. Addison Wesley, August 2007.

GPU Accelerated Scientific Computing: Evaluation of the NVIDIA Fermi Architecture; Elementary Kernels and Linear Solvers

Hartwig Anzt, Tobias Hahn, Vincent Heuveline and Björn Rocker
Engineering Mathematics and Computing Lab (EMCL)
Karlsruhe Institute of Technology (KIT), Germany
{hartwig.anzt, tobias.hahn, vincent.heuveline, bjoern.rocker}@kit.edu

Abstract—**This study compares the latest GPU generation of NVIDIA, named "Fermi", to the previous generation with respect to their performance in scientific computing. Both the consumer version of the hardware, GeForce GTX480 and GTX280, as well as the professional line, Tesla C2050 and C1060, are taken into account. The experiments include benchmarks of elementary kernels as well as of linear solvers applied to problems arising in the area of computational fluid dynamics. The study shows a raw performance gain of up to 50 % for the Fermi generation, while the GPU memory technology plays a central role for overall performance and energy efficiency in more data-dependent applications.**

I. INTRODUCTION

Recently, the number of users and lines of code taking advantage of the computational power of accelerators, especially GPUs, grew enormously. One reason is the facilitated programmability of GPUs by OpenCL and NVIDIA's CUDA. As early as 2003, several papers described the solution of the Navier-Stokes equations for incompressible fluid flow on the GPUs [1], [2] or other boundary value problems [4]. With the introduction of full double precision support on GPUs, many more scientific projects started porting their algorithms to GPU hardware.

An analysis of a meteorological simulation for tropical cyclones based on finite difference and an implementation of rigid particle flows using finite element techniques using GPU hardware can be found in [3]. As these studies demonstrate, hardware-aware numerical mathematics is a research area of high potential. Both, software and hardware have to develop hand-in-hand to yield highest performance and allow simulation and optimization algorithms to reach higher levels of detail and accuracy - A fact that is reflected in the development of our in-house finite element package HiFlow [11], that is able to use different kinds of accelerators.

In fall 2009 NVIDIA released their new chip architecture "Fermi" [7]. This study compares the performance of this new architecture to former generations, indicating the path of GPU development and its implication on scientific computing. In this paper, we benchmark basic BLAS routines for evaluating the raw chip performance of the GPUs. In order to measure the impact of the on-board memory technology during the interplay of different kernels, we also present performance results of a CG solver for a sparse system, resulting from a finite difference discretization of the Laplace equation. Larger parallel applications often need to communicate with the host, that is why we finally include results of a mixed precision GMRES solver that is partly executed on the CPU.

II. HARDWARE AND SOFTWARE ENVIRONMENT

We have chosen four graphics cards in total for this evaluation, two of the current and two of the former chip generation, where of each, one is from the NVIDIA professional line (Tesla) and one from the consumer line (GeForce). The chip and on-board memory specifications are given in table I. The main improvements to the first generation are an increased number single (MADD) and double precision units, and the introduction of GDDR5 memory with significantly higher clock rates. The latter is the reason for a 25 % higher energy consumption of Tesla C2050 compared to C1060.

Access to the graphics chips is currently only possible via PCIe, that is why the whole system configuration has to be taken into account when interpreting benchmark results. Not all test could be conducted on site, such that the system characteristics differ. The Tesla cards where benchmarked on Xeon systems that achieved similar PCIe saturations as the Core i7 Tesla with GTX280. Only the device-to-host rates differ a little for the non-pageable memory we are using for our tests. The GTX480 could only be tested on a workstation with an older chipset that merely achieved about half of the PCIe transfer rates. Details on the systems are given in table II, together with measured memory transfer rates and their saturation when performing operations with large vectors.

III. NUMERICAL EXPERIMENTS

With the above mentioned introduction of built-in double-precision support and furthermore IEEE754 compatibility, GPUs evolve towards universally usable processing units. Still, their paradigm is related to former graphics stream processing: The same series of operations is applied to every element of a set of data (i.e. a stream). Operations of a kernel are pipelined, such that many stream processors can process the stream in parallel. The limiting factor in this context is memory latency, especially when data dependency is high and data locality is low. GPUs try to hide memory latency by executing many kernel instances in parallel on the same core. Switching these

Name	Tesla C2050	Tesla C1060	GTX480	GTX280a
Chip	T20	T10	GF100	GT200
Transistors	$3 \cdot 10^9$	$1.4 \cdot 10^9$	$3 \cdot 10^9$	$1,4 \cdot 10^9$
Core frequency	1.15 GHz	1.3 GHz	1.4 GHz	1.3 GHz
Shaders (MADD)	448	240	480	240
GFLOPS (single)	1030	933	1.345	933
GFLOPS (double)	515	78	168	78
Memory	3 GB GDDR5	4 GB GDDR3	1.5 GB GDDR5	1 GB GDDR3
Memory Frequency	1.5 GHz	0.8 GHz	1.8 GHz	1.1 GHz
Memory Bandwidth	144 GB/s	102 GB/s	177 GB/s	141 GB/s
ECC Memory	yes	no	no	no
Power Consumption	247 W	187 W	250 W	236 W
IEEE double/single	yes/yes	yes/partial	yes/yes	yes/partial

TABLE I

KEY SYSTEM CHARACTERISTICS OF THE FOUR GPUs USED. COMPUTATION RATE AND MEMORY BANDWIDTH ARE THEORETICAL PEAK VALUES.

Host				Device				
CPU	MEM [GB]	BW [GB/s]	H2D [GB/s]	GPU	MEM [GB]	BW [GB/s]	D2H [GB/s]	CC ECC
2 x Intel Xeon (E5520, 4 cores)	32	12.07	PA: 3.25 PI: 5.86	Tesla T20	3	BT: 91.28 daxpy: 82.5 ddot: 88.3	PA: 2.51 PI: 4.75	2.0 Yes
2 x Intel Xeon (E5450, 4 cores)	16	6.14	PA: 1.92 PI: 5.44	Tesla T10	4	BT: 71.80 daxpy: 83.1 ddot: 83.3	PA: 1.55 PI: 3.77	1.3 No
1 x Intel Core2 (6600, 2 cores)	2	3.28	PA: 1.76 PI: 2.57	GTX480	1.5	BT: 108.56 daxpy: 135.0 ddot: 146.7	PA: 1.38 PI: 1.82	2.0 No
1 x Intel Core i7 (920, 4 cores, SMT on)	6	12.07	PA:5.08 PI:5.64	GTX280	1.0	BT: 111.54 daxpy: 124.3 ddot: 94.81	PA: 2.75 PI: 5.31	1.3 No

TABLE II

SYSTEMS' CONFIGURATIONS. THE ABBREVIATIONS ARE AS FOLLOWS: MEM IS THE AMOUNT OF MEMORY, BW THE BANDWIDTH, H2D DENOTES THE HOST TO DEVICE BANDWIDTH VIA PCIE AND D2H THE OTHER TRANSFER DIRECTION, CC IS THE 'CUDA COMPUTE CAPABILITY' AND ECC DEPICTS THE AVAILABILITY OF ERROR CORRECTING MEMORY. PA MEANS PAGEABLE MEMORY IS ALLOCATED PI DENOTES THE USAGE OF PINNED MEMORY.

lightweight "threads" and operating on other register sets can be done in just a few cycles, whereas the cost of fetching data from the global memory extends several hundreds of cycles.

While the problem described above is often inherent for many-core computing, other restrictions of stream processing techniques have been addressed in CUDA [7], which offer e.g. gather and scatter operations on the global graphics memory. The here evaluated chips can all be programmed with slightly extended C and runtime libraries, including hardware support for double precision, even obeying IEEE754 completely in the newest generation. As outlined in section I, we perform benchmarks for some elementary kernels in a first step, namely dot-products, vector updates, scalar-products, matrix-vector and matrix-matrix operations both in single and double precision. As our background is numerical simulation and optimization, our goal is to solve problems applying sophisticated mathematical methods. Hence, we rather aim at future compatibility than for optimizing low-level routines on single hardware generations. The tests are thus conducted using the same CUBLAS 3.0 routines, provided by NVIDIA.

In the second step, we evaluate the performance of a CG solver applied to a stencil-discretization of the Laplace equation, where we use own code for the sparse matrix routines.

Finally, we apply mixed precision iterative refinement solvers to linear systems arising in the field of fluid dynamics. These implementations use the GPU as well as the CPU of the host system, enabling us to give a performance evaluation of a more representative application.

A. Elementary Kernels Performance Evaluation

Figures 1 to 5 show the benchmark results of elementary kernels. The operations on vectors are clearly memory bounded, as the number of computations is low, and data cannot be re-used. The performance gain of 30 % in average from one generation to the other is thus mainly due to the improved on-board memory technology. Also, the difference from the consumer to the professional line is proportional to the memory clock difference. In the case of the GTX480/C2050, the factor is even larger, possibly due to the ECC protection.

The single-precision matrix-vector benchmarks show speedup proportional to the increased MADD-number. The same applies to the single-precision matrix-matrix benchmarks where each card, achieves about one third of its theoretical peak performance.

Most interesting are the double-precision results, where we observed two phenomena. Firstly, the C2050 cannot really

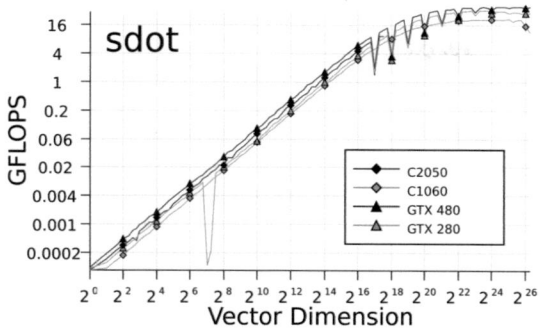 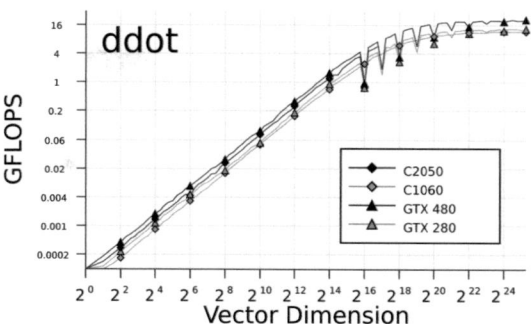

Fig. 1. Performance of the dot routine performed in single (sdot) and double precision (ddot).

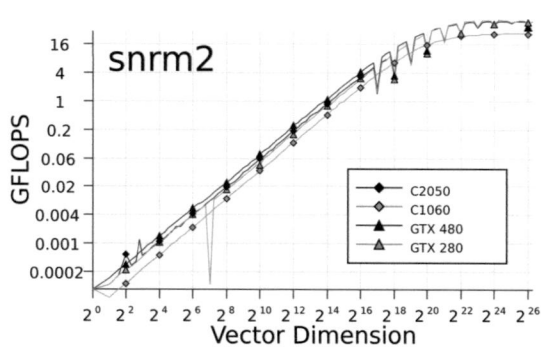 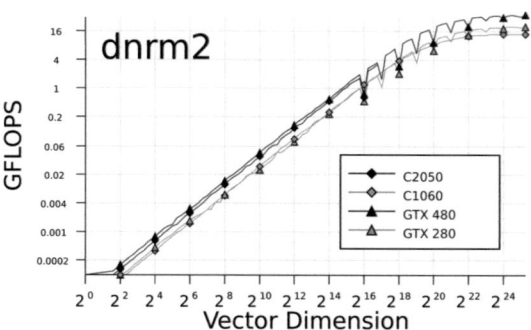

Fig. 2. Performance of the 2-norm routine performed in single (snrm2) and double precision (dnrm2).

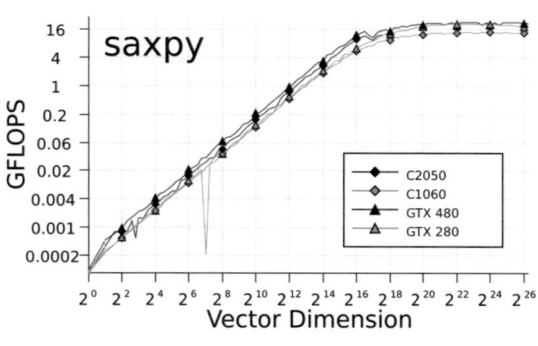 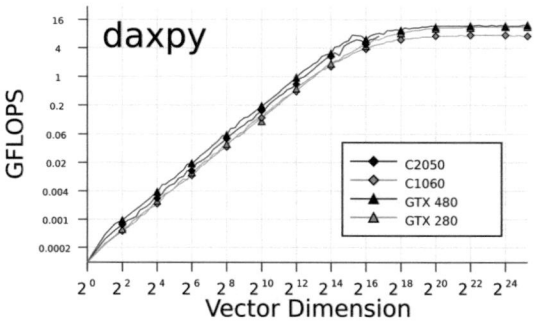

Fig. 3. Performance of the vector scale and add routine axpy performed in single (saxpy) and double precision (daxpy).

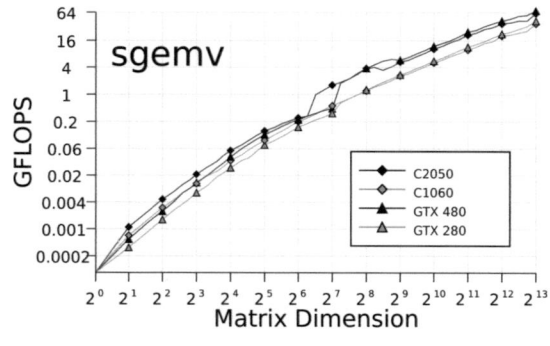 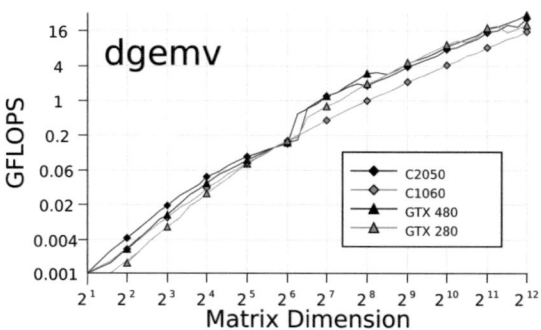

Fig. 4. Performance of dense matrix-vector multiplication routine performed in single (sgemv) and double precision (dgemv).

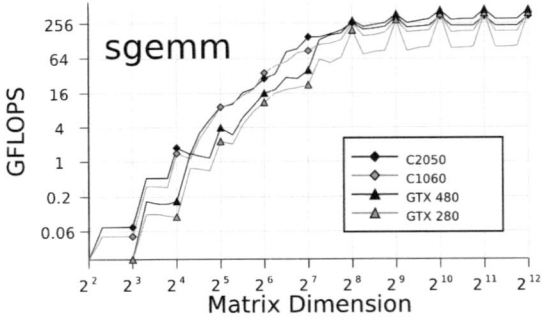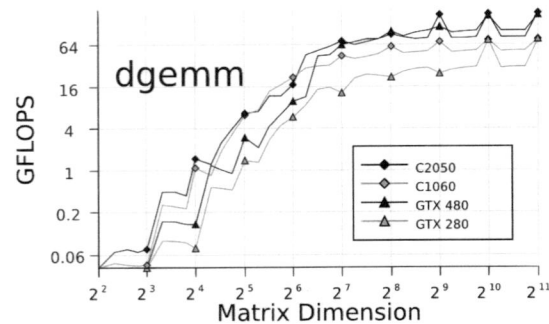

Fig. 5. Performance of the general matrix-matrix multiplication routine gemm performed in single (sgemm) and double precision (dgemm).

Experiment Setup		Performance (GFLOPS)			
Routine	Data size	C2050	C1060	GTX480	GTX280
sdot	185364	9.27	6.50	12.36	8.24
sdot	39903170	29.83	18.41	38.17	29.11
ddot	110218	5.38	3.50	6.68	4.16
ddot	39903170	18.79	11.03	19.38	12.48
snrm2	185364	7.72	4.88	9.76	7.41
snrm2	39903170	44.34	26.47	48.72	48.99
dnrm2	110218	3.06	1.79	3.39	1.79
dnrm2	39903170	22.74	13.49	33.22	19.22
saxpy	185364	11.96	8.62	14.83	11.23
saxpy	39903170	23.83	13.23	22.08	19.16
daxpy	110218	6.68	4.59	7.87	5.80
daxpy	39903170	12.54	6.92	11.33	10.52
sgemv	8192	58.19	34.63	68.72	40.49
dgemv	4096	25.39	14.74	29.69	19.52
sgemm	4096	330.17	367.61	430.40	368.75
dgemm	2048	174.21	74.40	161.97	73.76

TABLE III

PERFORMANCE FOR THE ELEMENTARY KERNELS FOR SPECIAL DATA SIZES.

Routine	Unit	C2050	C1060	GTX480	GTX280
ddot	ms	0.73	0.77	0.44	0.68
ddot	GB/s	88.28	83.33	146.78	94.81
ddot	GFLOPS	11.03	10.42	18.35	11.85
dscal+daxpy	ms	1.85	1.92	1.15	1.29
dscal+daxpy	GB/s	51.89	50.10	83.26	74.71
dscal+daxpy	GFLOPS	4.33	4.18	6.94	6.23
dcsrgemv	ms	18.70	19.59	11.53	13.15
dcsrgemv	GB/s	17.10	16.33	27.75	24.34
dcsrgemv	GFLOPS	2.14	2.04	3.47	3.04
daxpy	ms	1.16	1.15	0.71	0.77
daxpy	GB/s	82.55	83.41	135.02	124.35
daxpy	GFLOPS	6.88	6.95	11.25	10.36

TABLE IV

PERFORMANCE EVALUATION OF ELEMENTARY KERNELS OF THE CG-ALGORITHM ON THE FOUR EVALUATED ACCELERATORS. ALL MEASUREMENTS ARE PERFORMED IN DOUBLE PRECISION.

stand out against the GTX480, although its theoretical peak performance is three times higher and secondly, all but the C2050 almost reach their peak performance in the dgemm benchmark, while the C2050 drops to the ration of one third as for sgemm. A reason for this is not known to us, results provided by NVIDIA using the preliminary CUBLAS 3.1 on C2050 are in the same range.

For easier understanding of these findings, table III shows selected results out of the figures 1 to 5. Small data sizes are chosen in order to cover influences of latency, which seems to be equal for all cards. Larger data sizes measure the available bandwidth/computing power.

B. CG Solver

The second benchmark stage focuses on an implementation of the conjugate gradients algorithm (see e.g. [5]) based on the CSR data format. The linear system is obtained from a finite element discretization of the Laplace equation on a unit square using linear test-functions, which is equivalent to a finite differences discretization based on the 5-point-stencil. The matrix has the following characteristics: 4,000,000 degrees of

freedom (dofs) and 19,992,000 nonzero entries (nnz).

All computations are executed exclusively on the GPU and are performed in double precision, the absolute stopping criterion for the residual is set to 10^{-6}. Again, we avoid to optimize for one specific hardware platform, but use the CUBLAS kernels in version CUBLAS 3.0 as much as possible. Since the it does not contain any kernels for sparse matrix-vector operations, we use an implementation of *dcsrgemv* following the guidelines suggested in [6]. Optimizing the code for the different generations of hardware accelerator technology would result in higher performance, but at the same time limit the portability of the application and therefore make comparisons more difficult.

The performance results of the itemized kernels within the CG algorithm are presented in table IV, the complete runtime of the solver on the different GPUs is plotted in figure 6.

Again we see unexpected results for the C2050. While the GTX480 can clearly outperform the former GTX280 model for *ddot* and achieve an overall speed-up of 10 %, the factor between C2050 and C1060 is only 1.05. Also, the consumer cards achieve overall speed-ups of more than 1.5 compared to the professional versions, whereby even the older GTX280 is faster than the C2050. This is especially surprising as the specifications in table I indicate the opposite.

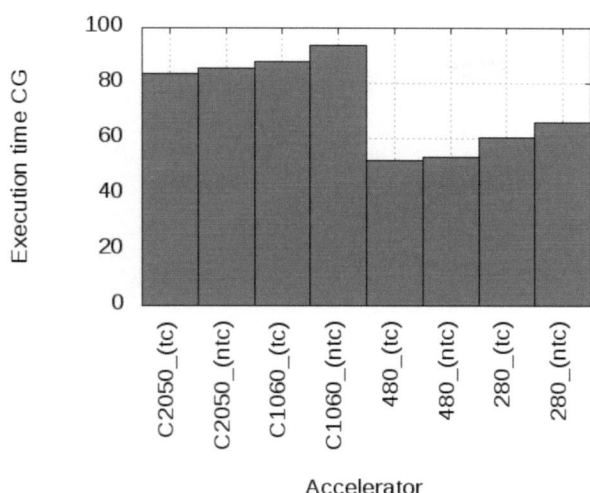

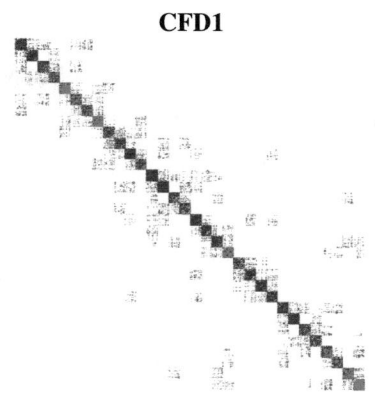

CFD1

problem: 2D fluid flow
matrix dimension: $n = 395009$
sparsity: $nnz = 3544321$
storage format: CSR

Fig. 6. Runtimes of the CG algorithm of the Laplace test for the four evaluated accelerators. *tc* results make use of texture caches, *ntc* does not.

C. Iterative Refinement Method

To be able to evaluate the computational power of the hardware platform in a more complex application, we use a GPU-implementation of a plain GMRES-(30) solver and a mixed-precision iterative refinement implementation based on the same solver. Mixed precision iterative refinement solvers use a reduced precision floating point format for the inner error correction solver, and therefore are able to exploit the often superior single precision performance of GPUs and the double precision performance of the CPU [8], [9], [10].

Both, the plain double GMRES-(30) and the mixed precision variant solve for the right vector hand side $\equiv 1$ with initial guess 0, using the relative residual stopping criterion of $\varepsilon = 10^{-10} \parallel r_0 \parallel_2$, while we choose $\varepsilon_{\text{inner}} = 10^{-1} \parallel r_i \parallel_2$ as relative inner stopping criterion for the error correction variant.

In the case of the mixed precision iterative refinement implementation, the error correction solver is executed on the GPU, while the solution update is performed by the CPU of the host system. This enables us to address larger problem sizes, since the available memory on the GPU is usually small compared to main host memory.

As test problems, we chose three systems of linear equations CFD1, CFD2 and CFD3, originating from a 2D Venturi Nozzle problem, discretized in different resolutions using Q2/Q1 finite elements. The distinct number of supporting points leads to different matrix characteristics in terms of dimension, sparsity, and condition number.

When comparing the total needed computation time, as given in table V, the Tesla C2050 performs better for small problems than the C1060 and the GTX280, but not as good as the GTX480. For large problems, the C2050 system outperforms also the GTX480. The explanation for this resides in the employed host hardware setup for the GTX480, where the memory bandwidth between host and device (PCIe) becomes the limiting factor for large problem sizes.

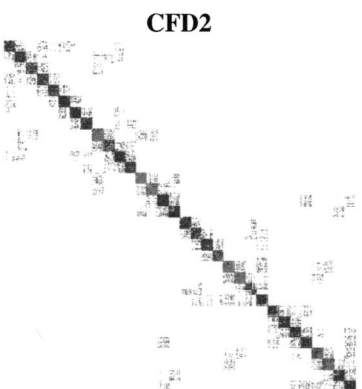

CFD2

problem: 2D fluid flow
matrix dimension: $n = 634453$
sparsity: $nnz = 5700633$
storage format: CSR

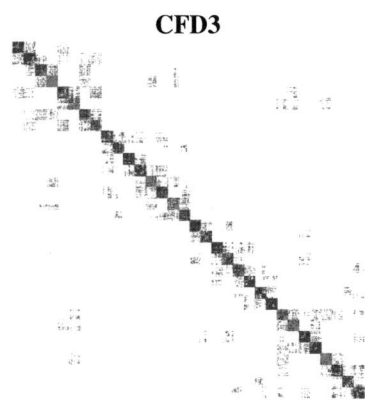

CFD3

problem: 2D fluid flow
matrix dimension: $n = 1019967$
sparsity: $nnz = 9182401$
storage format: CSR

Fig. 7. Sparsity plots and properties of the CFD test-matrices.

IV. REMARKS ON ENERGY EFFICIENCY AND ECC

Besides the computational performance, energy efficiency becomes more and more important for customers from academia and industry. In figure 8 we therefore present energy consumption estimates based on the theoretical peak power consumption of the accelerated systems given in table II and the runtime for our CG solver. In the case of the GTX480, the higher GPU performance does not come with a much higher energy consumption, resulting in the fairly good results. The unexpected bad performance of the C2050 in the CG test and its much higher energy consumption compared to the older C1060 caused its fairly poor test results.

The remaining main advantages of the C2050 are thus the more reliable hardware, which does support ECC. As this already requires lower clock rates, we decided to evaluate the necessity of using error correction code at all. We therefore implemented a test program, performing a matrix-matrix and matrix-vector multiplications using the CUBLAS routines over and over. The tests ran in parallel to a CPU-only implementation for a time period of seven days. During this test, we did not observe a single cache bit error, neither on the C1060 nor on the GTX480. This indicates, that also the cards without ECC are very reliable, though we cannot simulate data center production operation. Of course, for critical applications requiring ECC, there is no alternative to the C2050.

V. CONCLUSION

The current GPU generation offers enormous potential that can be utilized not only in synthetic examples, but also CFD applications with academic and real-life background. An essential condition for this is, that the underlying mathematical model combined with the numerical schemes for solving it offers enough parallelism to create a sufficient number of threads for the GPU to hide waiting time for memory calls of one GPU-thread by executing another thread. Exchanging threads is cheap compared to the time a global memory operation takes. The programmability of NVIDIA GPUs was heavily simplified by the introduction of CUDA compared to the most common former approaches. Due to this, significant performance increases can be achieved in very short time by e.g. extending existing applications with accelerated kernels in Fortran and/or C/C++, like the partially ported meteorological implementation in [3] shows. Highest performance is achieved when porting the code completely to the GPU and thereby

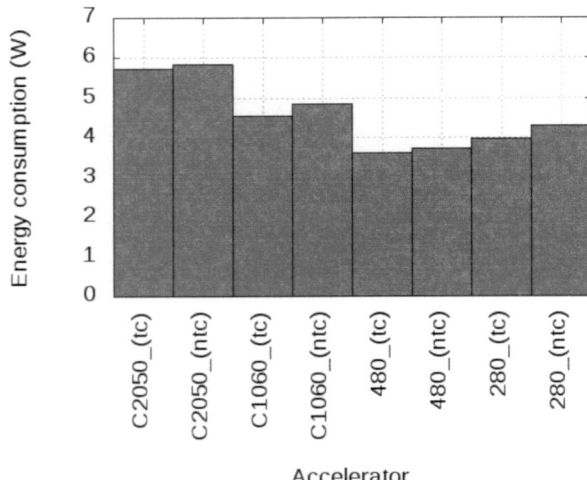

Fig. 8. Energy consumption in Watt hours (Wh) of the Laplace test of the four evaluated accelerators. *tc* employs the texture cache, *ntc* does not.

avoiding host-device communication as much as possible. The new generation of Tesla and GeForce accelerators based on the Fermi architecture offer an additional gain in computational performance already by looking at the theoretical values compared to the previous generation. For many kernels and applications based on such kernels, the performance can be used in practice, as this study demonstrates, though we did not observe the jump in double precision performance of the new Tesla line, we had hoped for. When memory bandwidth is the limiting factor, the speed-ups are lower again, due to the fact that the memory bandwidth did not increase to the same ratio as the ALU count (see table I). Still, the measured speed-ups are in a range of 1.2 for the CG-algorithm, because of the newer memory standard (GDDR3 vs. GDDR5). Similar results can be achieved for the mixed precision iterative refinement solvers, though the speed-up decreases for larger dimension, as then the PCIe memory bandwidth becomes the bottleneck. The energy efficiency tests reveal that the performance gain in terms of execution time of the new Tesla generation comes with the price of a significantly higher energy consumption. The consumer versions show much better test results in this category. In this respect, it should be mentioned, that besides the floating point performance this paper focuses on, the resilience of hardware is equally important in cluster computing.

Experiment setup		Computation Time (s)			
problem	solver type	C2050	C1060	GTX480	GTX280
CFD1	plain double GMRES-(30)	164.84	252.74	145.23	183.37
	mixed precision GMRES-(30)	80.48	129.19	60.98	98.46
CFD2	plain double GMRES-(30)	473.38	778.75	456.17	518.49
	mixed precision GMRES-(30)	273.99	510.38	256.43	301.41
CFD3	plain double GMRES-(30)	993.63	1921.64	1145.08	1046.49
	mixed precision GMRES-(30)	554.28	1555.36	669.57	697.12

TABLE V
COMPUTATION TIME (S) FOR PROBLEMS CFD1, CFD2 AND CFD3 BASED ON A GMRES-(30).

The rather high performance of the consumer cards comes with an uncertainty in terms of correctness of long-lasting computations as especially the memory components are not designed for reliability. The importance of ECC could not be evaluated conclusively in this study and is a topic of further investigation.

ACKNOWLEDGEMENT

The authors would like to thank Werner Augustin and Dimitar Lukarski from the Shared Research Group (SRG) [12] for their assistance while performing the benchmarks and his contributions for the content of this paper.

REFERENCES

[1] Bolz, J., Farmer, I., Grinspun, E., Schröder,P.: Sparse matrix solvers on the GPU: conjugate gradients and multigrid. ACM Transactions on Graphics, vol. 22, 2003, pp. 917-924

[2] Krüger, J., Westermann, R.: Linear algebra operators for gpu implementation of numerical algorithms. ACM Transactions on Graphics, vol. 22, 2003, pp. 908-916

[3] Hahn, T., Heuveline, V., Rocker, B.: GPU-based Simulation of Particulate Flows with CUDA: Proceedings of the PARS Workshop 2009, German Informatics Society, 2009

[4] Goodnight, N., Lewin, G., Luebke, D., Skadron, K.: A multigrid solver for boundary-value problems using programmable graphics hardware. Eurographics/SIGGRAPH Workshop on Graphics Hardware, 2003, pp. 102-111

[5] Saad, Y.: Iterative Methods for Sparse Linear Systems, 2nd edition: SIAM: Philadelpha, PA, 2003

[6] Bell, N., Garland, M.: Efficient sparse matrix-vector multiplication on CUDA: NVIDIA Technical Report NVR-2008-004, December 2008

[7] NVIDIA: NVIDIA's next generation CUDA compute architecture: Fermi, v1.1: Whitepaper (electronic), September 2009. www.nvidia.com/content/PDF/fermi_white_papers/NVIDIA_Compute_ Architecture_Whitepaper.pdf

[8] Anzt, H., Heuveline, V., Rocker, B.: Mixed Precision Error Correction Methods for Linear Systems: Convergence Analysis based on Krylov Subspace Methods: Proceedings of PARA 2010 State of the Art in Scientific and Parallel Computing, 2010.

[9] Anzt, H., Rocker, B., Heuveline, V.: An Error Correction Solver for Linear Systems: Evaluation of Mixed Precision Implementations: Proceedings of VECPAR 2010 High Performance Computing for Computational Science, 2010

[10] Anzt, H., Rocker, B., Heuveline, V.: Energy efficiency of mixed precision iterative refinement methods using hybrid hardware platforms: Computer Science - Research and Development, Springer Berlin / Heidelberg, 2010

[11] Heuveline, V. et al.: HiFlow - A Flexible and Hardware-Aware Parallel Finite Element Package: EMCL Preprint Series, 2010. www.emcl.kit.edu/preprints/emcl-preprint-2010-06.pdf

[12] Shared Research Group (SRG), Karlsruhe Institute of Technology (KIT), http://www.numhpc.math.kit.edu

List of Authors

Financial support

The Shared Research Group (SRG) 16-1 on *New Frontiers in High Performance Computing Exploiting Multicore and Coprocessor Technology* is a joint initiative of Karlsruhe Institute of Technology and Hewlett-Packard. The SRG receives grants by the Concept for the Future of Karlsruhe Institute of Technology in the framework of the German Excellence Initiative and by the industrial collaboration partner Hewlett-Packard. The present proceedings of the Second International Workshop on New Frontiers in High-performance and Hardware-aware computing are kindly sponsored by the SRG.